MY HUSBAND THE CHEAP BASTARD

By David Kuoch and Amy Gayheart

Copyright © 2009 David Kuoch

Retired Hipster is a registered trademark of Retired Hipster, Inc.

Some of the material in this book originally appeared, occasionally in different form, in the blog My Cheap Bastard Husband (http://mycheapbastardhusband.wordpress.com)

Library of Congress Cataloging-in-Publication Data available.

ISBN: 978-0-9822977-1-1
First edition

Manufactured in China.

Book design and layout by Gayheart Design
Copy Editing by Cory Bilicko

Thank you to everyone who has shared a story about their spouse in order for us to laugh a little harder.

10 9 8 7 6 5 4 3 2 1

Retired Hipster, Inc.
PO Box 14068
San Francisco, CA 94114
www.retiredhipster.com

INTRODUCTION

The following stories have been submitted by real women– wives who are fed up with the cheap ways of the men in their lives. The women in this book continually try to outdo each other in detailing the true stories of what their Miserly Misters will go through to save a buck. This is not a "how to" guide, but an exposé, shining light on the techniques and stories of these anonymous "Kings of Thrift."

IS YOUR SPOUSE A:
MISER?   CHEAPSKATE?   SCROOGE?
CHEAP BASTARD? TIGHTWAD?
PENNY PINCHER?

Is your husband one of these men? Does he make a game out of trying to save money? Are you tired, stressed out and embarrassed by the lengths your husband will go to save a dime? Or at the end of the day, are you just glad he has a little extra money saved up to take care of you? Does your husband, like some of the men in these stories, frequently cross the line between spendthrift and mental patient?

Find out for yourself, as you laugh out loud when you hear what these ladies have to say, and you can be the judge of who is a "keeper," and who is just "cheaper."

THE 99-CENT STORE ADDICT

Like anything in life, the dollar store has its time and place. I usually find a reason to fit the dollar store into my weekly shopping routine. The dollar store can be a treasure trove of little knick-knacks, and a miscellaneous grab bag of cheap, useful, all-purpose products. Let's say you're in a fix because you're having a kitchen emergency. You're in a pinch for time, you need a spatula, and you need it soon. Well, why pay a premium on a fancy, brand-name "spat" when the dollar store is right across the street?

Like most people, I find value in the dollar store. But my husband...he takes it too far. He's always trying to save a buck and, for him, that place is like Xanadu. My husband is a dollar-store addict.

As he walks around the store, he'll become entranced by the thousands of available, inexpensive items, each one making a compelling pitch as to why he should purchase it. Hypnotized by the rock-bottom deals on toys, candles, cake mixes, rainbow-colored plastic bowls, silver underwear, tea lights, squirrel soaps, lighters, and enough candy to kill a Girl Scout troop with terminal diabetes, my husband will use each one of these amazing deals he's getting as a point of departure to go on a manic out-of-control spending spree.

He'll spend as much at the dollar store in one day as we spend in a week at the grocery store. At least when we go to the grocery store we have food to show for ourselves afterwards. I mean, what are we going to do with six sets of extension cords, nine packages of industrial-strength moth balls, an entire set of pineapple-shaped plastic cups with an accompanying bundle of Hawaiian-themed paper plates, and 16, I repeat, 16 packs of unopened pro-rated golf balls? We certainly can't eat any of these things. They're just taking up space in the garage.

Maybe I should have a yard sale one day while my husband's at work and sell all this junk. I can open up a competing "Everything for 50 Cents" store on our front lawn and get a small portion of our money and dignity back from these dollar-store crooks.

This sounds like a pretty bad situation, right? Well, guess what. What I told you so far was the light side of things. The money doesn't even really bother me so much as the deplorable quality of the products he brings home.

I was so mad at him the last time I sent him to the store. I'd given him a very specific list that included: toilet paper, tampons, shampoo, and cat litter. I even told him which brands he should try to get if they were on sale.

He pretended to listen as I went over the list a second time. The whole time he kept nodding and groaning comprehension at me. The stingy bastard knew he wasn't going to get any of the brands I asked for. He was planning from the get-go to cheap out and go to the dollar store.

I'm sorry, but there are some things you just can't cheap out on. It's not worth saving a dollar if your toilet paper is coarse and scratchy like sandpaper. How much value do you get out of tampons that cost a dollar, in their diseased-looking, brown wads of cotton from a Third World country (which by the way, I'd never put in my body)? Is it worth it to save four dollars on cat food if the cats are up all night yowling bloody murder with a stomach ache and vomiting all over the carpet?

I personally believe shampoo should only be spelled with one "a." When my husband brought home a bottle of "shaampo" from the dollar store last week, it was the last straw.

"There's no way I'm putting that stuff on my hair! I could become a mutant!"

"He'll spend as much at the dollar store in one day as we spend in a week at the grocery store."

"Come on," he argued, "it's just shampoo. They're all the same.
You're brainwashed by the commercials."

"Okay, you're banned from the dollar store," I said.
"You've lost your dollar-store privileges."

"But I..."

"Nice doing business with you." I patted him on the shoulder and pushed past him out of the living room.

These days when I send my husband out to the store, I give him an exact list of the brands and products I want. I look up the sale items online in advance. Then, when he gets home from the store, I pocket-check him for a receipt. If I find him hiding any 99-cent knick-knacks, any mini gadgets, appliances or doodads that we don't' need, I'll tell him, "You better start looking for a '99-Cent Lawyer,' cause we're through, buddy!"

– Monica, Beverly Hills CA

"Dumpster diving for goodies"

CRUMBS OF CONTENTION

We're all familiar with the term and concept "baker's dozen," whereby the bakery owner gladly adds one more item to the anticipated 12. It's always nice to get one extra doughnut, cookie or roll, but my cheap husband Ray takes this idea about 10 steps forward and asks for a "beggar's dozen."

He is the king of asking for expired baked goods, every time we go to our neighborhood bakery. It typically goes something like this: We walk in together, hypnotized by the smells and sights of all the goodies, and, as I get lost in perusing the glass cases for freshly baked croissants and dinner rolls, my husband some-how makes his way to the back of the store, looking around and inquiring about day-old bread. After some haggling, he cuts a deal.

After one trip there, I walked out with a small, pink box of immaculately deco-rated petit fours intended for a dinner party dessert, and he quickly drove up in our car, telling me to hop in. Ten minutes later we met the baker out by the dump-ster behind the restaurant. That's right, I said the dumpster! The baker handed my husband two black trash bags full of baked goods, and my husband gave him ten dollars. If you ask me, my husband overpaid him for taking his garbage off his hands.

When we arrived home my frugal spouse opened up the bags to reveal about 15 loaves of bread, 50 corn muffins, 70 rolls and 30 baguettes. "What are we going to do with all that?" I asked.

"Eat it!" Ray answered, as if it was a stupid question.

There wasn't enough room to store it all, so he went out and bought an extra freezer. To save a few pennies, he spent almost $200. And for about six months, he happily ate his free bread with just about every meal. Now that he is 15 pounds heavier, he's beginning to rethink the idea of having all this bread around.

Now he's on a diet, and I don't let him eat goods from the bakery anymore; instead, he's now befriending our nearby produce managers for their less-than-fresh fruits and veggies.

– Chrissy, Anaheim CA

THE BOTTOMLESS CUP

My husband Arnold is about one cup of coffee away from getting his walking papers. I swear, I'm going to send him packing. The funny thing is we met in a Starbucks. This was just a few months ago. He looked so smart sitting in the coffee shop, reading my favorite author– Ernest Hemmingway. It was love at first sight, and we got married a couple of weeks later. Little did I know what I was getting myself into...

It just goes to show that you shouldn't make important decisions in your love or life until after you've had your first cup of coffee in the morning.

Like many people who work for a living, Arnold likes to start his day at the Starbucks with a jolt of caffeine. The difference between him and everybody else? He doesn't pay for it. Not full price anyway. What my husband does is exploit a loophole in the Starbucks refill policy.

Whereas a normal cup of coffee begins with a $2 price tag and can cost upwards of $5, a refill only costs fifty cents. My husband uses the same paper cup over and over again. He'll walk into the store with a ragged, stained, flimsy cup that looks like something a homeless person fished out of the garbage. He'll walk right up to the counter and ask for a refill with his fragile cup. Hello! Like they're not going to notice. I mean, come on, have you no shame? Have I no shame? I married the guy!

My idiot husband will use the same cup three, four, maybe five times, until it's completely deteriorating and decomposing right in his hands. It's disgusting.

You'd think my husband would stop when his cup finally falls apart, but there's no stopping him. What he does is pay for the refill and ask for a "cup-in-a-cup." He uses the pretense of the cup being too hot so he can ask for a second cup as insulation. He wants two cups! And the barista will say, "Sir, if your coffee is too hot, I can give you a 'sleeve'." "I don't like the sleeves." My husband will start to make a stink. "I want another cup." And nobody wants to have a scene, so he gets his way. As if he's fooling anyone! I half hold the coffee shop employees responsible for his behavior. They don't stop him! They're enablers!

> "I know that a lot of marriages are ruined because of drinking, but it's not usually because of drinking coffee."

The Starbucks employees are onto him though. They're not stupid. They stare at him with a look that says, "Here's your cup, now please, just shut up and stop holding up the line." The Starbucks manager one time even called him out by name. The manager was only half-kidding when he looked at my husband and said, "So, when was the last time you paid full price for a cup of coffee, Mr. Jones?"

My husband was stunned.

"How the hell do you know my name?" he asked.

"Because you're the guy who charges fifty cents to his debit card every morning," the manager answered.

My husband looked down at his feet, having been caught red handed. I cleared my throat and nudged him with my elbow. "Um... ok... sorry," my husband grumbled as he took out his wallet. His eyes wavered between the bills in his wallet and the tip jar on the counter. He wanted to buy his way out of trouble.

To my surprise, he put his wallet away and reached into his trouser pocket. I was so mortified when he finally came up with a whole quarter and dropped it into the tip jar. Like this manager was going to be bought off for twenty-five cents? What a cheap-ass!

The worst part is that when I confronted him about the cups, he claimed an ecological defense. He tried to take the moral high ground by telling me he was recycling. He even tried to turn the situation back around on me, by essentially saying that I was being irresponsible by not stealing coffee.

"I want you to pick right now," I demanded. "It's either me or the Joe."

Nowadays, my husband's on his best behavior when we go into coffee shops together. But, he's only one soiled, recycled cup away from being a bachelor. I know that a lot of marriages are ruined because of drinking, but it's not usually because of drinking coffee.

– Linda, Seattle WA

THE PLASTIC BAG HOARDER

It can take years to really get to know a person– maybe even a lifetime. About a year ago I found out something about my husband Tony that I wish could forget.

One time I was digging through the cabinets in our house when I came across his plastic bag "collection." I know what you're thinking– most people save their plastic bags. Well, my husband's plastic-bag hoard was like nothing I'd ever seen before. His bag stash could have been a roadside attraction, like the world's biggest ball of twine, or a "mystery spot."

He had bags from every conceivable store known to man sculpted into a crumpled plastic ball in our cabinets.

After that, I started to notice Tony's bag problem all the time. A few weeks later, we were in Target at the self check-out. He rang up his items and then paid the bill like a normal person. No problem. He looked back at me and smiled nervously. Then, just when he thought I wasn't looking, I saw him do the unthinkable. Like lightning, he made a move for a whole cache of extra plastic bags, and quickly stuffed the whole stack into our grocery bag.

"What are you doing?" I quietly chided him.
"What? It's okay. You're allowed to take extras."
My husband was shoplifting! Plastic bags! How crazy is that?
"What are you going to do with all those bags?" I asked him.
"That's an awful lot of bags."

"What do you mean? I use them."

"Sure you do," I said. "You use them to clutter up the cabinet."

"I use them as trash bags. Why pay for trash bags when you can get them for free?"

"Are you serious?" I folded my arms across my chest and shook my head. Cheap bastard.

"Never you mind about the bags," he said, as he tried to nonchalantly make his escape.

After that incident, I dreaded going shopping with him. It seemed like every single time I went to the store with him, he would either ask the check-out clerk for extra bags or he would just pocket them right there like they owed it to him. There was no stopping his bag lust.

"Why pay for them when you can get them for free."

I reached my tipping point once I discovered that, during more than three years of marriage, every time my husband would go to the grocery store, he would drive 15 minutes across town to the Shop-4-Less because it's easier to steal bags from there. We live right next to a grocery store! For three years, I just thought he was the slowest shopper on the planet!

I finally got so fed up with his bag thieving that, on his birthday, I stole off with his whole plastic bag collection from the cabinet. I dumped the lot of them into a recycling bin far away from our house just in case he tried to find them. Who knows how many years of his life he'd spent saving up and hoarding these bags?

I went to the store and bought a box of trash bags. I wrapped the box up like a present and stuck a big red bow on top of it. "You like free bags so much?" I said, as he opened the gift-wrapped package of trash bags. "Well, happy freaking birthday!"

– Susan, St. Paul MN

ART AND FREEBIES LOVER

One of the reasons I fell in love with my husband was his love for culture and the finer things in life, particularly when it came to art. We met ten years ago at a gallery opening in the city. He looked so refined and sophisticated standing with his cute little plate of cheese and crackers. He seemed to be studying this one sculpture so closely, so carefully, that it was as if he was another sculptor trying to figure out how to replicate the original. One thing led to another and we ended up having a great conversation comparing Monet and Matisse. We started dating and he took me to more art openings. It was a romantic, picture-perfect courtship; and, to make a long story short, we fell in love and got married.

So, you'll understand my shock when I found out that my husband isn't even interested in art.

I had started to notice a pattern. Over the years, whenever I'd ask him if he wanted to take me out to a gallery, he'd always ask me the same exact questions: "What kind of opening is it?" "Which gallery was it?" "Do you think they will have food?"

If I told him that a certain gallery or show didn't have free food and drinks he'd refuse to go! Cheap schmuck that he is, my husband has been going to art openings for the free refreshments! Our entire relationship and ten long years of our lives have been completely predicated on a lie!

Who knows? Maybe, at one time, he did appreciate the art. But now my husband's idea of having a good time at an art gallery is hovering around the buffet table like a vulture. We used to go out to dinner before we'd go and hit the art scene. Now the art scene **is** dinner!

It's gotten to the point where I don't even want to be seen at a gallery with my husband. As soon as we walk through the door, he makes a beeline for the snacks and I head in the opposite direction. I try to play it off like I came in alone.

I finally reached my saturation level when we went to this really nice gallery in the city a few months ago. Within ten minutes he had already downed two glasses of wine and three shrimp puffs. Fifteen minutes later: four glasses, five shrimp puffs, and two spinach pies. At thirty minutes: an entire bottle of Pinot, five shrimp puffs, five spinach pies, and three egg rolls. Believe me, I was counting every agonizing second, every painful snack, as I stood by in shame and watched him gorge. He feasted from the trays of stuffy, bowtie-wearing waiters like they were his own personal coffee tables.

The whole time the room was so crowded and my husband was standing so close to me that I couldn't even pretend "I'm not with this man!"

After consuming a seemingly inhuman amount of free food, probably a third of the gallery's entire food budget, my husband went to a place I never thought he'd go. "Excuse me," he said, as he pulled one of the waiters aside. "Can I get some of those shrimp puffs wrapped up to go?" "Um…" uttered the poor waiter, who didn't know what to say. "Gee, I don't think so."

I tapped my husband on the shoulder to get his attention. "One second," he told me and put up his finger to stop me. "I'm talking to someone."

"I'll be in the car," I informed him.

"It's gotten to the point where I don't even want to be seen in public at a gallery with my husband."

On my way out of the gallery, I saw a man wearing a black shirt and glasses, standing in front of and admiring an Impressionist painting. He reminded me of my husband ten years ago. Only this man wasn't holding a plate of food.

I was so mad at the time, I'd actually considered trading in my husband for a new, better model.

– Erica, Brooklyn NY

WHO ORDERED EXTRA BUTTER?"

When you go out to dinner with a group of friends, does your husband ask to split the bill? Every single time?

If you answered yes to both these questions, then he's probably a cheap bastard like my husband Frank.

Every time I go out to a restaurant with my husband, it's a nightmare. Okay, he's not the guy who pulls a dine-and-dash and skips the check. He's not a criminal. But when it comes time to pay the check, he's just as bad as a criminal. Sometimes, I think I'd prefer it if he was breaking the law. It might be slightly less embarrassing.

"He'll itemize every last line of the receipt."

It doesn't matter whom we're out with– friends, family, business colleagues, etc. If he can't get a separate check, Frank will sit there in front of everyone and itemize every last line of the receipt. He refuses to pay any more than his exact mathematical portion of the bill. And since he's always ordering cheaper food than everybody else, he always has an excuse to make a big "to do" when he refuses to pay for someone else's "fancy" filet mignon or "swanky" swordfish.

"Honey," I'll try to reason with him, "just pay the bill so we can leave." He'll rudely point across the table at one of our good friends. "So I guess it's my fault her majesty had to have the sea bass?"

It would be one thing if it were about the money. But my husband makes a very decent living as a civil engineer. We're not hurting, that's for sure. And to boot, he's the son of two very proper, very prim Ivy-League professors. You'd think they would have taught him proper table etiquette!

Frank and I have only been married a year. He always paid for dinner when we were dating so I had no clue he was like this. It wasn't until about three months ago that I first noticed the extent of his cheapness. We were at a birthday dinner for his best friend, Jake– a large table of 15. As usual, it made sense to just divide the bill up equally. That's what regular people do anyway.

When the waitress came around to take my husband's order, he told her he wanted a separate check for himself. Everyone thought my husband was joking, even the waitress.

No one took my husband seriously until the evening was winding down and the house came to collect. Everyone threw in $35 regardless of their order except my husband, who decided to cough up $8 for the chef salad, and $2 towards the tip. Every other person at Jake's birthday dinner, including me, pays $35, and my husband comes up with only $10?! He didn't even pay for my meal! We even had to recalculate the amounts each person needed to chip in, since Frank threw a wrench into our system of efficiently getting the bill paid. And he calls himself Jake's best friend. Some best friend. Some husband.

I'm just glad that we don't go out a lot. I don't think I could deal with the stress. Maybe, for my husband's next birthday, I'll throw him a big surprise dinner, and then stick him with the check.

– Blair, Dallas TX

CONCESSION STAND CON

I started dating my husband over 15 years ago when we were both in college. At the time we lived on strict budgets and cut a lot of corners to save a buck or two. We would scour local papers for coupons, and look for the cheapest happy-hour specials at all the bars and restaurants in our area. We also used to sneak food into the theaters whenever we'd go out to see a movie.

Lots of college students sneaked food into the movies. It was fairly common. We'd go to a movie with several of our friends, and we'd all have our contraband snacks hidden in our pockets and pocketbooks, under our shirts, jackets, coats, and scarves.

The movies back then cost $5, which was a lot to us, considering that we went to the movies every week. It made sense for us to sneak in stuff like bottles of Yoo-hoo, M&Ms, and Milk Duds, since we just didn't have the extra money to patronize the concession stand.

Fast-forward to 15 years later. My husband and I are all grown up. We have a house and two fairly new cars. We both have our own businesses. From an outside glance, my husband would be virtually indistinguishable from a normal, well-adjusted adult.

Except for this one little tic...
Fourteen years, three months, and 11 days since we got married, and my crazy, cheapskate husband still to this day refuses to pay for popcorn or any movie snack for that matter! I'm not saying that we're crawling hand over fist with money, but we're certainly comfortable. We certainly don't have to sneak food into the multiplex like unruly teenagers.

My husband's justification is based on principle, and he refuses to make any "concessions" at the extortion-priced concession stand.

If he was just sneaking a couple of small things in, then I could really care less (although I don't really care for the crunching sound he makes with the nuts). But it's not just a little candy. He takes it to the next level. He'll often pop his own popcorn and smuggle it in. But that's the least of his transgressions. He'll bring just about any food on Earth into the movie with him: chicken chow mein, submarine sandwiches, even ice cream. One time he took three slices of pepperoni pizza and folded them all in half like napkins. He crammed the slices into a zipper sandwich bag and then stuffed the bag into his back trouser pocket, on the side opposite to his wallet.

A couple of weeks ago, he actually wanted me to hide a Styrofoam container full of leftover hot wings in my purse.

> "...Just throw it in your purse,
> nobody will notice."

"There's no way I'm taking those wings in my purse!" I told him.

"Come on, just do it! I'm going to be hungry halfway through the movie!"

"So buy something there."

"You know I won't do that. Come on, just throw it in your purse, just for a few minutes."

"Put it in your own purse," I told him.

"Fine... I'm getting my backpack."

It was about that time that I picked up the latest issue of *TV Guide* from the coffee table, to see if there were any shows worth staying in for.

– Susan, Denver CO

FREE FOOD ON AISLES
1 THROUGH 10

My husband Gary is big cheapskate with a capital "C." His dad was a cheapskate, as was his father before him. And Gary certainly follows in their footsteps.

As a gag gift for his birthday, our daughter bought him a T-shirt that said, "I'm a cheapskate and proud of it!" Guess what. He was proud of it! He wore that stupid shirt all over town like it was some kind of designer name brand.

Instead of making lunch at home or going out to eat as normal people do, my husband will troll around the big warehouse grocery stores like Costco and Sam's Club, looking for a free meal. He'll literally go around from one free sample station to the next, until he's eaten as much or more than most people who have paid good money at a restaurant would get from a normal meal.

When we go to the store, my husband is like a bird of prey spying a small rodent in a field. He spots baby-back ribs, little hot dogs, or barbecued chicken wings from across the store. As soon as I see that look on his face, I know what's going to happen: Let the feeding frenzy begin.

My husband has a cheap but effective strategy for getting free samples. He'll be polite and super friendly, chatting up employees and customers alike, as he shamelessly feasts on an entire tray of bite-sized servings. The servers at the free-food tables usually don't care who's taking what from their stations, even if they see a cheap freeloader like my husband coming back for seconds or even thirds... or fourths or fifths.

I'm just saying that at some stores people can make an entire meal out of the samples. The weekend is usually the best time to go if you're feeling up to braving the crowds.

I, on the other hand, will never, ever go to Costco again with my husband on the weekend. Our last trip to Costco was the proverbial straw that broke the camel's back.

As I did the shopping, my husband of course was looking for his meal ticket. I was walking through the frozen-foods section when I overheard a commotion at the end of the aisle, over by the display case where they usually keep the free samples.

"Oh, God," I thought. "Please don't be my husband."

"That's right, you're eighty-sixed."

It was my husband.

I found him at a sample station, arguing with an elderly lady conservatively dishing out tiny triangles of pizza.

"Look, lady, just give me the pizza," I heard my husband say.
"Young man," the elderly woman shot back.
"This is your sixth slice of pizza in 10 minutes."
"You must be mistaking me for someone else."
"Young man," she said, "I may be old, but I'm not blind..."
"Come on, lady," he said.
"That's it!" the old lady said. "You're eighty-sixed."
"Eighty-sixed?" my husband asked.
"That's right. You're cut off. No more free samples for you."
"I demand to speak to a manager right now."

As my husband continued to bicker, I hastily made my escape through the back of the aisle. I left the shopping cart half-full and took off through the sliding glass doors into the parking lot. I couldn't show my face in that Costco anymore. I didn't want anyone to see me with my husband.

I got into my car and pulled out of the parking lot without looking back. Fifteen minutes later, my cell phone rang. It was my husband finally calling to find out where I went.
"How was the pizza?" I asked him.
"It was fine," he said.
"Well, that's great," I said.
"By the way... have a nice walk home."

I had hoped that this incident would have some effect towards dissuading my husband, but the very next day he was back at Costco hitting up the same sample tables again. Seriously, is there some kind of support group where he can get help? When's the next Food Samplers Anonymous meeting?

– Adria, Marina Del Rey CA

I WANT IT MY WAY, OVER AND OVER

When my husband and I went on our first date, he took me to a fancy restaurant in the city. At the time, it was one of the most expensive restaurants in the area, and I was very impressed.

I remember that we both ordered these incredible "surf and turf" steak and lobster dinners. Everything was just about perfect: the food, the wine, the company, until about halfway through dinner when my husband noticed a tiny piece of hair on his steak.

He called over the waiter and complained. To make a long story short, my husband got his meal for free. Pretty typical scenario so far, right? Many people have experienced this type of situation in a restaurant, at least once.

What you might not expect, however, is that since that first date, my husband has tried to pull this same stunt every single time we've ever gone out to dinner. He does it on purpose.

It's the same thing every time. He'll eat 70 to 80 percent of a meal and then find something wrong with it. The food will be too cold, too overcooked, too under-cooked, too spicy, or not spicy enough.

"There's something wrong with every single meal out there," my husband tells me. "You just need to know what to look for."

He'll call over the waiter, and then the manager if he has to. Nine times out of 10 though, they'll either comp his meal, or give him a coupon or gift certificate for a free meal the next time he comes in. My husband's not exactly a great actor or anything. It's just that from the restaurant manager's point of view, it's not worth the headache to fight him. The aggravation coupled with the risk of getting a bad word-of-mouth reputation creates a situation where my husband gets away with murder. Apparently, there's no stopping him.

I've tried to call him out on his behavior. He says it's just a game. A game? He should be arrested for what he does.

The most annoying part is that we don't even need the money. My husband's an orthopedic surgeon, for Christ's sake!

"Something about it doesn't taste right."

My husband is so cheap and so shameless he'll even pull the same crap at fast-food restaurants. Seriously! He'll eat 80 percent of a burger and then have the chutzpa to take it back up to the counter to complain. They'll give him a refund or exchange it for something else. Even at McDonald's the schmuck will get his burgers two for the price of one. It's as if he's above the law.

It's gotten to the point where I just won't go out to eat with him anymore. However, there's one place he eats where he knows better than to even consider sending back his food....... my kitchen!

– Mary, Emeryville CA

THE THIEF OF CABLE TV

Let me begin by stating, for the record, my husband and I are not poor. We both have good jobs, limited debt and a decent amount in savings.

Nevertheless, you wouldn't know it to walk into our living room. Whereas every other household in this neighborhood (believe me, I checked) has a new, flat, 54-inch (or larger) plasma-screen TV sitting in their family room, our TV is like something you'd find in a dumpster. It's from the early 1980s and has rabbit-ear antennas rigged with a hanger. Rabbit ears! He's too cheap to fork over the money for cable. Our TV even has adjustable dials for sound and color contrast. Adjustable dials! Remember those from back in the day, before they invented the "button?"

My six-year-old son asked my husband why his little friends don't have rabbit ears at home on their TVs. My husband took him aside and sat him down in a chair. He looked at him seriously.

"Hold onto those rabbit ears, kid. They're going to be worth a fortune some day." I couldn't help but overhear the conversation. I had to step in to save my son.

"Why would those rabbit ears be worth a fortune?"

"They're vintage."

"Yeah, well..." I dug in and decided to take a stand on the issue, right then and there. Enough was enough.

"When that TV was built," I said, "they didn't have cable."

"Like cable's so great?"

"Phil, we only get four channels."

"20 to 50 bucks a month for cable really adds up!" he says.

> "Do you think the neighbors
> have an extra cable box?"

Never mind the thousands of dollars he spends every summer on that boat. And the rest of the year, it's just sitting around taking up space.

"I want cable, you cheap SOB!" I screamed.

"Fine," he said. "So we'll get cable already. Go ask the neighbors if they have a second box."

He wanted to see if we could hijack our cable off of our next-door neighbors' connection. Forget that it's embarrassing and un-neighborly. It's also illegal. I mean, what kind of example are we setting for our kids?

So the cheap son-of-a-gun finally agreed to get cable. And, after all that, he still somehow managed to cheap me out. Instead of paying for cable like a normal person, he hired an off-duty cable guy/contractor to come over and hook up our connection illegally. My husband even slipped the guy an extra 50 to hook up all the premium channels. All of them! And that bribe was a one-time fee!

Okay, so maybe Mr. Cheapo is not so bad after all. I should give him credit where credit's due. He's an excellent negotiator. And, after all, I am enjoying all the free movies on the premium channels...... that is, until the cops come knocking.

- Samantha, San Francisco CA

THE CONDIMENT MAN

My husband is a condiment con man. He won't pay $3 for a bottle of ketchup at the grocery store. Nor will he pay 99 cents for a bottle of ketchup at the dollar store. He won't spend a single penny on any kind of food that he can steal little packets of when we go out to eat.

When we go to a fast-food restaurant, and all the condiments are sitting there in one place, free for the taking, they're like fish in a barrel when my husband's around. He'll stand there and stuff his pockets with handfuls of ketchup, mustard, even salt and pepper.

I mean, okay, everybody takes condiments from a restaurant. It's not so bad, right? But my husband takes it beyond far. He'll even steal the plastic utensils.

I'll ask, "What do you need those for? We've got a silverware drawer at home!" And he'll tell me, "We'll use 'em for a picnic or a barbeque. Besides...dish soap isn't free, you know. The money we'll save on mayo can be spent on the things we can't get for free here."

His favorite things to pilfer are the little moist towelettes that come in the square wrappers. Not only are they hand sanitizers, but they double as an all-in-one, all-surface cleaning tool. They're the only cleaning product he'll use when he's cleaning the windows in his car. He also loves the creamers and the sugar packets. If you were in our kitchen, and you opened one of our cabinets, you'd think we owned a restaurant franchise!

When we're at a restaurant, my husband will try and encourage the kids to go nuts with the never-ending condiment reserves. I swear to God, I could kill him sometimes. "Hey, kids," he told our children a few months ago when we went out to eat, "don't be afraid to use a little of that sugar. Get your money's worth."

Whatever packets they don't use my husband will put in a bag. One day he walked out of a restaurant with an extra "to go" bag full of nothing but packs of mayonnaise, lemon juice and tartar sauce! I was so grateful no one we knew was there that night.

"You'd think we owned a restaurant franchise!"

Can you believe El Cheapo will sometimes go to a fast-food restaurant just to make off with the condiments? He won't even buy anything. He just walks in and starts pocketing condiments.

One time he even brought a plastic container with him from home and filled it up with ketchup from the industrial dispenser at the McDonald's near us. A store employee saw what he was doing and tried to intervene.

"Sir, you can't do that."
"What do you mean I can't do that? I'm being environmentally conscious." My husband picked up a stack of empty paper condiment cups to show them to the poor restaurant worker. "You know how many trees died to make these things?"

The unfortunate guy didn't know what to say to that. He stood there quietly and let my husband abscond with all the ketchup he could get into his container.

Open our refrigerator and you'll see more condiments than there is food. And you'd think, with our condiment surplus, we'd never have to worry about ketchup, sugar, nondairy creamer or salt again. But you'd be wrong.

When we go out to eat, it's "go nuts with the condiments." When we get home though, my husband rations the condiments out, two per person. I swear to God, I couldn't make this up. He's like the Gestapo with those sugar packets!

I guess the saddest part is the impact it's had on our kids. Since they don't get to use much of the stolen condiments at home, they tend to go a little overboard when we are elsewhere. Last week, I took them to a local burger joint (without their father) and let them use as much ketchup, mustard and mayo as they wanted. When my five-year-old daughter took her first bite of her cheeseburger, the red, yellow and white gunk practically shot out the other side of it!

– Lily, Anaheim CA

RETURN TO SELLER

Despite being a substitute teacher and living on that modest salary, my husband Ron always seems to have the latest and most impressive high-tech gadgets.

His friends are amazed that he's consistently able to stay on the cutting edge of new technologies. But I know his dirty little secret. My charming, loving spouse is a compulsive "short-term customer." That means he'll buy a big-ticket electronics item, get less than 30 days of use out of it and then return it.

It's an annoying habit, though it never really bothered me much. What do I care if he wants to buy a new Blu-Ray player and then return it? He takes meticulous care of his gadgets before returning them to the store. So...I don't really think it's a moral issue. It's something that I certainly would never do. So I'm married to a "short-term customer." I made peace with it. That is...I had made peace with it until recently.

For Christmas this year, Ron bought our family a top-end, home video camera. It was such a great gift. We were able to capture our three kids unwrapping their presents, our New Year's Eve party, and a few weeks later, we recorded our daughter's 12th birthday party.

Then, 30 days later, like the Ghost of Christmas Past, Ron came to repo the video camera, so he could return it to the store.

"You can't do that," I told him. "This was a present! Not a short-term buy!"

"Do you know how expensive that camera was? Do you want me to get another job? Because that's what I'll have to do if we keep that camera."

So...we agreed to return the camera. What could I say? It was fun while it lasted.

The next day while Ron was at work, I was getting ready to run some errands and I saw the camera sitting boxed up on the table with the receipt on top of it. I figured I'd go ahead and return the camera while I was out.

> "... I'm praying this does not get into the wrong hands."

When I got back later Ron looked really scared.

"What's wrong?" I asked him.

"Where's the camera?"

"I returned it," I told him. "Isn't that what you wanted?"

"Did you, um... uh..." he tried to ask, while nervously peeling the label off a bottle of domestic beer, "... delete what was on there?"

"I didn't, no. I figured you would have already done that, being that this whole return system was your brainchild."

He just put his face down into his hands and shook his head. I guess I did feel really sad about it. I mean, all those precious memories, down the toilet! Just then, a sudden flash of recollection hit me. I could feel my face turn white, and my breath freeze in my lungs.

"But you did at least delete the video we made after the New Year's party.....right?" I asked, hopefully.

Ron put his face down, this time onto the bare tabletop. That was all the answer I needed. I blacked out and fainted.

Now, thanks to my cheap husband, our big, local, corporate electronics store has video of me, wearing nothing but a thin spread of peanut butter and whipping my husband. We're just...you know...praying it doesn't get into the wrong hands. Or for that matter simultaneously aired on 20 bigscreen TVs in the electronics store.

– Dawn, Austin TX

THE EXTENDED WARRANTIES KING

Technology comes and goes so fast these days. Just when you think a gadget or a computer is "new and exciting," they come out with a "newer and more exciting" model that you simply must have.

After going through this never-ending cycle of buying new computers and gadgets every year, my husband has found a loophole to level the playing field. He's found a way to make the extended warranties on purchases work to his advantage.

When you buy an item at the electronics store, it automatically comes with a manufacturer's warranty that provides you with very little real coverage. But you can get an extended warranty that offers you more coverage by paying a premium, sometimes ten to twenty percent of the cost of the original item.

Well, my husband always purchases those extended warranties and you better believe that he's going to get his money's worth. When the warranty is about to expire, my husband will call the manufacturer or electronics store and work them until he gets his item fixed, or even better, replaced. For example, my husband bought a laptop and then, three years later, when the extended warranty was just about to expire, he called to say that the hard drive was acting up even though there was nothing wrong with it. The company replaced the laptop, no questions asked.

Another time my husband was able to get upgraded to a brand-new printer since the older model was out of production. It's hard for me to keep track of all the warranties my husband is milking, but it seems like every six months he has a new cell phone.

I know that many people view extended warranties as scams because some electronics companies make you jump through hoops just to get them to resolve your issue. I've heard all the warranty horror stories. For some reason, my husband's never had any problems. Maybe that's because he's the one running the scam. Maybe my husband is the horror story that the customer service reps complain to each other about when they get off work.

He calls himself "The King of Extended Warranties." What a nerd. He swears that he knows all the extended warranty policies of all the major electronic stores and manufacturers by heart. He's read all the fine print, so he knows exactly what is and is not included in a warranty.

"I'm pretty sure that's borderline fraud," I told him.

"What's the point of having a warranty if you're not going to use it?" he asked.

The scary thing is, the more I think about it, he seems to be right. Maybe I'm the crazy one.

– Sandie, Sarasota FL

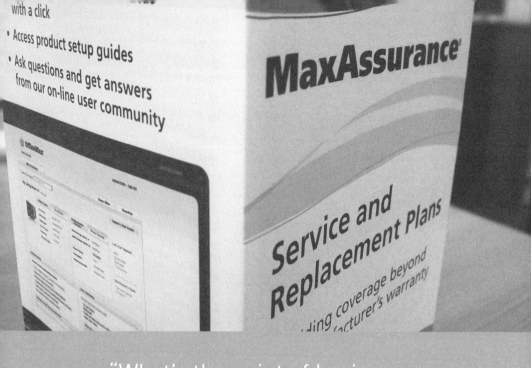

with a click
- Access product setup guides
- Ask questions and get answers from our on-line user community

MaxAssurance®

Service and Replacement Plans
...ding coverage beyond
...acturer's warranty

"What's the point of having a
warranty if you're not going to use it?"

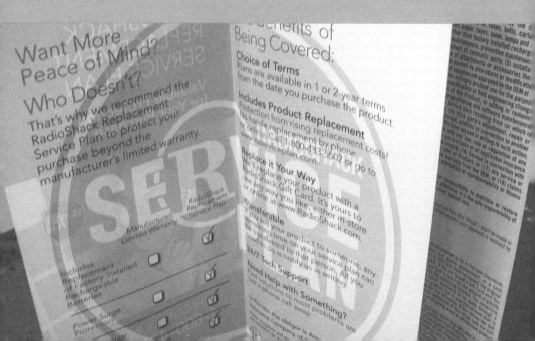

Want More
Peace of Mind?

Who Doesn't?
That's why we recommend the
RadioShack Replacement
Service Plan to protect your
purchase beyond the
manufacturer's limited warranty.

Benefits of Being Covered:

Choice of Terms
Plans are available in 1 or 2-year terms
from the date you purchase the product.

Includes Product Replacement
Protection from rising replacement costs!
No hassle replacement by phone
or online. Call 1-800-433-5502 or go to
www.rsserviceplan.com.

Replace it Your Way
We'll replace your product with a
RadioShack Gift Card. It's yours to
use any way you like; either in-store
or online at www.RadioShack.com.

Transferable
If you sell your product to someone, any
remaining time on your service plan can
be transferred to that person. All you
need to do is notify us in writing.

24/7 Tech Support
Need Help with Something?
Fast solutions to most problems are
just a phone call away.

"I don't think it's copyright infringement."

KINKO'S TEXTBOOK MANUFACTURING MAN

I call my husband the Textbook Manufacturing Man. He hates to pay full price for books, so he goes to Kinko's and photocopies entire books from cover to cover. I mean, I know we all did that in college. But my husband does it to this day! And he's supposed to be some kind of a grown-up.

Let's say that a book costs $30 in the bookstore. Well, the cheap bastard will buy the book and photocopy it, then return it, even if it costs him $25 to make it happen! He doesn't care that he only saves $5, or that he probably wasted more than that in gas driving over to Kinko's. And then it takes him a half hour to an hour to photocopy the book. And let's not forget about the time he wastes sitting in traffic before he even gets back to the store.

It's absolutely insane; it has become his addiction. I almost wish he were using drugs instead. It would be easier to find treatment for him. What's the methadone equivalent for Xerox dependence?

Not long ago we were at my husband's friend's house for dinner. My husband came across a book on his friend's shelf.

"Could I borrow this book for about an hour?" my husband asked his friend.
"Going to do some speed reading?"
"Not exactly," my husband replied.
"Sure, I don't care."

My husband, right there and then, took off to Kinko's. He ditched both me and his friend for a copy machine! I didn't even know his friend all that well. He left us alone together for over an hour. I was so beyond mad.

When he got back, I chewed him out.

"You cheap son-of-a-bitch! Did you have to do that now? Why can't you borrow a book like a normal person? Have you ever heard of a library?"

"But why would I want to read a book that 17 other people have handled, that's full of their germs? Plus I don't get to keep it. This way, I can add to my collection of literature," he suggested.

When you walk into most people's homes, you see bookshelves neatly lined with hardbound books. However, a trip into our home "library" produces row after row of manila folders..... full of photocopied books.

- Susan, Anaheim CA

THESE BOOKS ARE MADE FOR RETURNING

I met my husband at a secondhand bookstore in Berkeley. He was wearing stylish glasses and designer shoes, sitting on a bench reading a book about Cicero. Being the diehard bookworm that I am, I was interested in him right away and admired how he seemed to be lost in his own world.

We struck up a conversation and it turned out that we were both visiting from San Francisco for the day. He was a lawyer, and he was visiting a guest lecturer at the university who happened to be my old college roommate.

He gave me a call when he got back to the city and we started dating. Because we both loved to read, it didn't really matter that almost every single one of our dates took place in a bookstore. We would just hang out together and read inside the store. It felt comfortable. It felt right. I was in love.

We married a year later. I thought I had the "perfect" guy. After a while though, I started to notice something odd. My husband was always so careful with the books he bought. I couldn't understand why. He wouldn't open a paperback book all the way as he read it because he didn't want to put a crease in the book's binding. Even more peculiar was his habit of reading for five hours in a row and then putting the book back in the plastic sleeve from the bookstore. I thought it was kind of funny but everybody has quirks, so I never questioned him about it.

Except, one day, I was sitting at the table eating some dark chocolate and drinking a glass of Merlot while reading a book he'd purchased the day before. Since I needed one hand to eat and drink with, I was holding the book with the other, and I had the pages folded back so it was easier to hold.

When he entered the room and got a gander at the red wine, chocolate and the way I was handling the book, he lost it.

"Don't do that!" He rushed toward me, but slowly and carefully pried the tome from my hands. "Oh, it's ruined. I guess it's ours now! Thanks a lot."

> ## "He didn't want to put a crease in the binding."

He left the room, and I was bewildered.

The next day, we were browsing through different areas of a local independent bookstore when I overheard one employee whisper to another, "The Book Returner's here today."

"Where?" the second employee asked, almost excitedly, as if the circus were coming to town.

"The history section," the first employee said.

I knew the truth before I looked, but I had to find out for myself. Standing there where "The Book Returner" should have been was my husband. He was the only person standing in the entire history section.

My husband was a Book Returner!

When I confronted him he broke down and confessed. He admitted to bringing back all the books he'd bought after reading them. He would buy a book, power through it in a marathon sitting and then return it.

"What about all the ones in our library? Why did you keep those?" I pushed him.

"Those were gifts from my mother," he answered.

Ever since that day I've bought all of my husband's books for him. I refuse to be known as The Wife of The Book Returner!

– Alexi, Marin CA

BLACK-EYED PETE

Going to see your favorite bands in concert is a luxury not many people can afford. Even the average concert fan sees only two a year. And forget about getting any kind of good seat for a show; that's beyond expensive.

I'm not that crazy about the loud music and the crowds, but my husband Pete somehow manages to see about 20 shows a year. And somehow he always seems to get the best seats. Since he's usually so cheap, I just couldn't understand how he could be scoring these amazing ticket deals all the time. And it turns out...he wasn't.

I finally discovered his angle when he took me to see the Black Eyed Peas as a surprise birthday present. The music for the opening act was great, but our seats were terrible. Maybe he had been exaggerating all this time about these so-called "great" seats he was getting. When the first band finished playing, Pete grabbed my arm abruptly.

"Let's go," he said.

"We're leaving already? We just–"

He yanked me up out of my seat and down the aisle. We booked out through the door and down three flights of stairs, practically leaping out onto the main floor seating area. We rushed to the eighth row, where he gruffly escorted me to two vacant seats in the middle. We planted ourselves and he relaxed.

"I have to hand it to you," I naively said to Pete "these are pretty amazing seats."

"And you doubted me?" he said.

"Yeah..." I admitted, "I thought you were so full of it."

"Hey! That's my seat!"

Two large, street-tough-looking chicks were standing in the aisle closest to our seats, and seemingly staring us down.

> "I can't understand how he could score these amazing seats."

I looked at them, trying to determine whether they were indeed referring to us. Pete looked away from them and pretended not to notice.

They made eye contact with me. I pointed to myself, questioning without sound. They pushed their way into the row.

"Get up!" the bigger one told us.

Pete stood up and played dumb, ready with a response. He pulled out his ticket and said, "No, I believe these are our seats."

A second later, the bigger of the two gigantic women socked Pete right in the face. He dropped to the floor. I helped him up and we quickly made our escape, gladly relinquishing the seats.

Back at our proper seats, the stage lights came back on, and I saw the damage done to Pete's face. Somehow, with one jab, she'd managed to give poor Pete a black eye and a nosebleed.

"Hey, honey," I said. "Is this why it's called the nose-bleed section?"

– Emily, Venice CA

OVERSTOCK

Whenever my husband sees a sign in a store advertising a product as "free with coupon," he will literally drop anything he's doing to drive to that store and pick it up. It doesn't matter what the product is, let alone whether or not he needs it. He likes to stock up. But you'd think he was preparing for the end of the world.

Sometimes, I'll admit, it's great. Since I love cooking, it's very convenient to have my husband constantly restocking the shelves with new ingredients. If I need a can of condensed milk, I'll always know that there will be one waiting for me in the pantry. I know that there are at least five packs of bread crumbs in my kitchen right now.

I definitely don't have anything against free stuff, so long as we need it. But what are we going to do with eight bags of dog food when we don't have a pet? Why would I want to have seven umbrellas when we live in the desert? What's the use of having a case of blank audiocassettes when we live in 2009? And what are we going to do with a case of condoms when we've been married for 12 years and he's had a vasectomy?

Some stores will place limits on how many free-coupon items a customer can get. Well, that doesn't deter my husband. He's found a way around it. He'll go through the trouble of driving to different store locations. One time, he went back to the same store twice; the second time he was actually wearing a disguise so they wouldn't recognize him.

I don't have the heart to fight him, but I am trying to break him of his habit. I've recently convinced him to donate hundreds of canned food items to a local soup kitchen. But there's much, much more where that came from. By the way, if anyone out there has any use for 15 copies of *The Da Vinci Code*, 12 bags of kitty litter, or 30 rolls of aluminum foil, please let me know.

– Francesca, Miami FL

"Let me know if you need anything."

BUY ONE GET ONE FREE

"Dinner is on you."

OURS IS FREE, ALL OTHERS MUST PAY

Everybody loves getting a great deal. One of the best promotions a store or restaurant offers is the "buy one, get one free" special. We all take advantage of them. Why not? But my husband Larry takes things too far.

After not having seen his sister Wendy in over three years, Larry graciously invited her and her husband Paul to accompany us to dinner. We took them to an upscale Thai restaurant that came highly recommended in the "gourmet" section of the weekend paper.

Larry and his sister joked about old times and we all enjoyed a good meal of pad woon sen, tom kha gai, and spring rolls. Then the check came, and Larry pulled out two "buy one, get one free" dinner coupons.

At this point, the normal thing to do would be to put the 50-percent discount towards the entire meal and then split the cost with our guests. Well, that's not what happened.....

Larry told his sister that since they didn't have any coupons, they should pay for both of their meals which, in this case, would be the entire meal.

"And then Gina and I will get our meals for free!" When they didn't seem to share his enthusiasm, Larry added, "Don't you get it? It's buy one, get one free. I have two of them!"

It was really quiet for about five seconds, as we three waited for Larry to break into laughter, signifying that, of course, it was all just a joke. But that never happened. My sister-in-law and her husband politely and quietly took out their wallets. Forcing smiles on their faces, they picked up the entire check including tax and tip. You'd think my husband would have at least offered to pay for tax and tip, which were not included in either of the coupons?

He didn't.

That was a year ago and Larry's sister hasn't talked to him since. Maybe the last time they got together, three years before that, was also at a restaurant.

– Gina, Houston TX

THE DISCOUNT MAN

In certain cultures and countries, bartering is the way business is conducted every day. In those parts of the world, buyers and sellers are constantly engaged in negotiation, haggling with each other over every single commercial transaction made. Obviously that's not the way we do things here in North America. Sure, there are some places where bargaining is deemed socially acceptable, like flea markets and yard sales; but for the most part Americans don't try to get 25 percent off a Big Mac when they order from the drive-through. By the way, my husband Steve doesn't mind making all the cars stuck behind him in line wait as he attempts to swindle a better price. He views the traffic backup as a bargaining chip in his favor.

I should have known what I was getting myself into on our first date. Granted, at the time, we were both in college, and we lived in a small town in Kansas, so...there weren't exactly a lot of choices as far as restaurants go.

Even so, he told me he was taking me out on the town to a fancy restaurant. He said that we were going to "paint the town red." You'll never imagine my surprise when we pulled into the Denny's parking lot.

"Is the fancy restaurant behind the Denny's?" I asked him, innocently.

"Come on, this is a nice restaurant. Did you want to go to Al's Steakhouse? That place isn't so nice. For one thing, Al is a huge womanizer..."

With my husband's superior negotiating skills, he managed to get me to concede it was a nice restaurant and sold me on the date. Eventually, he talked me into the marriage as well.....but that's another story.

When the Denny's waitress came over to take our order he blindsided her with requests and demands. He caught her off guard with his bartering skills. In her world, the price of a Grand Slam Breakfast had been solid, fixed and immutable. Until now...

"I saw this Denny's commercial on TV a few months ago for the $3.99 breakfast. I know the promotion's over, but I was wondering if we could get two of those. If not, then we're going to have to take our business somewhere else."

"Sir, I'm not sure..." The confused waitress scratched her head with her pencil.
"Look, I'm a regular customer. I come here all the time," Steve told her.
"Really? I think I'd remember you," the waitress tapped her leg impatiently.
"Look," Steve persisted. "Could I talk to a manager, please?"

The manager started to walk over from the counter.
He stopped cold when he saw Steve.

"What's all the commo—? Oh, no. Not you again!"

Steve turned to the waitress. "You see! I told you I was a regular!"

It was the first in a series of a lifetime of embarrassments. But, still, to my husband's credit he did get the discount.

At first I thought it was kind of cool that my husband could get discounts wherever we went. After all, who doesn't like a cut rate, right? And then the most amazing thing happened and it changed everything: I grew up and he didn't.

We live in Los Angeles now and my husband makes a comfortable six figures. Now he treats it like a game. Everywhere he goes, he is still haggling and bartering, and sometimes, it just makes me sick.

My husband will always, always, ALWAYS ask for a discount when he makes a purchase regardless of the location or the people around him. He'll ask for discounts at restaurants, grocery stores, bars, and coffee shops– anywhere money changes hands, he'll ask for a break. He'll even ask the people at the post office if he can get a discount on stamps! And they wonder why so many postal workers crack.

I have a theory that my husband will act like a crazy person on purpose to get his way. He'll rock the boat and make a scene until people bend to his will. Employees are terrified of him. Do you think some ill-prepared teenager can take on the bargaining master? Usually it's a massacre! He'll always come armed with some kind of rational argument to justify his behavior. Sometimes he'll claim that a product is damaged and that he's doing them a favor by taking it off their hands.

My husband can get discounts for all kinds of reasons. I've witnessed him inspecting shirts with a microscope in hopes of finding a missing button- or a pivotal thread that's loose- some small defect that gives him the legitimacy to march up to the sales clerk and ask for a discount. Steve really holds them over the coals if the item has been in any way opened or returned. I wouldn't be surprised if, when I'm not around, he damages the item or opens it himself, hoping to use that as a pretense to get the price knocked down.

Imagine my husband is in a department store and he's trying to score a toaster. If he's having any kind of problems whatsoever getting an uncooperative employee to play his game by his rules, he'll pull out the big guns. He'll take a giant wad out of his pocket and try to make them a cash offer.

"I know what the price tag says, guy," he'll say as he's counting out bills. "You don't have to tell me...I can read. But level with me, what's your real number? What's the bottom line?"

I'm almost certain that before my husband passes away, he'll go to the mortuary and barter for a discount on his coffin. And you know that if there is a heaven, my husband's talking his way in, through those pearly gates.

– Stacey, Los Angeles CA

FOREVER REFILLS

Not only is my husband cheap, he's also disgusting! Did I mention cheap?

Most of the time, I refuse to go out to eat fast food with him.

If you were to look into the back seat of his car, you'd see drink cups from every fast-food joint that offers free refills, which is most of them. He has this whole collection of used, soiled drink cups!

That's right, ladies. My husband is so damn cheap he refuses to pay one measly dollar for a soda.

Some of the cups in his car are weeks old. They're covered with dust and disgusting brown stains. It's completely unsanitary. Despite the appalling conditions of the cups, he still uses them to milk free refills from fast-food places.

If one of his cups gets too flimsy, he will stand beside the garbage and solicit people for their cups just as they're about to throw them away. Can you believe that?

Sure, when I've seen him do it, he took the cups home and washed them before reusing them. But who even knows what he's up to when I'm not around? For all I know, he could be taking the cups into the bathroom right there and rinsing them out with hand soap, or even worse, not washing them at all.

I mean, these people throwing away their cups could be diseased. They could have the plague, or some rare new contagious virus that no one's ever heard of before. My husband would take a cup from an outbreak monkey if he could. And he wonders why I don't like to kiss him on the lips. Yuck!

How does he get away with this? Good question. He has a system. He'll only go into a fast-food restaurant during the lunch or dinner rush when the employees are too busy to notice the "fountain burglar." Until recently, I hadn't accompanied my husband to a fast-food restaurant for over six months. The last time I did, he wanted me to share his drink with him. He refused to pay for a drink and I refused to share.

I swore I'd never go back to McDonald's with him again. The other day I finally broke down and went out with him to get lunch. It was well worth the trip. I finally got to see him get his comeuppance.

As we walked into the place, he had his cup in hand held at an angle behind his back. He was trying to be sly. There was only one employee in the dining area and she seemed to be preoccupied cleaning tables, so my husband let his guard down. He set his used cup down on a table and went into the bathroom.

As soon as he left, she walked over to his cup to investigate. She picked it up with the tips of her fingers as if it smelled awful (which it probably did) and grimaced.

Without any hesitation she tossed his contraband cup into the garbage.

When my husband came out of the bathroom, he searched for his missing cup, and I thought, "Finally! He's going to be shamed into never reusing those dirty cups again."

But he went over to the woman who was now wiping down another table. "Excuse me, but did you throw away my cup? I set it on that table there so I could use the bathroom," he said to her.

"The fountain burglar strikes back."

She seemed confused initially, but said,
"Oh, I'm sorry, sir. I'll get you another one."

As she left him to go behind the counter for a clean cup, I left him to go behind the wall to act like I didn't know him.

His obsession had just been reinforced with a new idea for acquiring free paper cups.....remove someone else's dirty cup from the trash, leave it on a table for a while as you use the restroom, then ask for a replacement when it gets discarded by an employee.

As demented as it might sound, I actually succumbed to this idea. At least he'll be drinking out of clean cups from now on!

– Amanda, Santa Ana CA

21

ONE SIZE DOESN'T FIT ALL

It's true, kids grow fast and plenty of parents do buy clothes that are bigger than their children's current sizes. That way, their kids will have room to grow into the new clothes. Normally, however, when people do this, they get their kids clothes that are only one size too big,

My darling hubby Mark, on the other hand, is so cheap that he buys clothes for our kids that are two to three sizes bigger than they should be.

Usually Mark hates going shopping, but for some reason he seems to enjoy buying our children plus-sized clothes. He figures that if he buys the clothes bigger the kids will wear them longer and we'll save money. What Mark fails to realize is that his whole concept is inherently flawed. First of all, our kids wear the giant clothes so long that they get worn out around the same time anyway. Second of all, the new clothes get dirty much faster since the kids are always dragging their long pants legs through dirt and puddles, or tripping over their oversized "clown shoes." My 11-year-old son's sneakers are so big he looks like he should be playing in the NBA.

So we have to buy our kids new clothes anyway. But, thanks to my husband, the kids get to walk around all day at school feeling awkward and uncomfortable.

I've pointed this fact out to him, but does he listen to me? No.

He still insists that our kids will grow into the clothes eventually.

When I go shopping for the kids, they turn out looking cute, because the clothes actually fit. When my husband buys them, they look as if they've been playing "dress up" after raiding my husband's and my closet. It's so ridiculous. I want to scream!

One day, things came to a head when I caught my husband snooping through my dresser drawers. He was holding an old blouse of mine up in front of him.

"What's going on here?" I asked, ready for the worst.

Nonplussed, he held up the blouse in front of a mirror.

"You're not planning to...wear that? Are you?"
I asked him, trying to not use my imagination.

"Of course I'm not going to wear it," Mark snapped.
"I was just trying to see if you had anything that might fit Lisa."

"She's seven years old!" I screamed at him.

"Exactly," he reasoned. "She's not getting any younger."

I couldn't take it anymore. I shook my head in disgust. His behavior was wrong on so many levels.

"Okay," I said, taking a deep breath. "From here on, I'm in charge of dressing our children."

"Come on, babe. I'm just trying to save us a little extra bread." He rubbed his fingers and thumb together.

"Okay", I took another deep breath. "Here's the deal. You worry about making us money; I'll worry about what the kids wear. In other words," I told him, "you earn the money, and I'll spend it."

"For some reason he enjoys buying our kids clothes."

"Fine," he grumbled, slinking meekly towards the doorway to leave the bedroom.
"Whatever...""Oh, and one more thing" I shouted after him.
"Stay the hell out of my drawers, freak!"

I think he got the message. Since then, he's laid off of shopping for the kids. However, recently, I did catch him looking down and examining his own shirt when he noticed that our son was wearing a shirt that was too small on him. When my son reached above his head, his shirt was so short that his belly stuck out.

My husband took off his T-shirt and checked out the size on the tag.

"Don't even think about it," I chided him and grabbed my son's hand.
"We're going shopping.....at a children's clothing store!"

– Senika, Aurora CO

22

PLASTIC MAN?

Most women look forward to going out to dinner with their husbands but I absolutely hate it. I would rather have a picnic in the park with an enraged colony of fire ants in the dead of winter than spend five minutes in public at a restaurant with my husband.

To save money when we go out with family or friends my husband will forgo ordering dinner. He'll lie and say he's not hungry or that he had a big lunch even though I know that it's a lie. I know it's a lie because I'm the one who makes his lunch, for Christ's sake. My husband the penny-pincher would never spend the money to buy a second lunch when he already had a perfectly good bag-lunch. It's a complete fabrication!

When they bring out the food to everyone else but my husband he will start picking off of everyone else's plates like a scavenger. The last time we went out to eat with my brother's family, my husband made a point of sitting next to their seven-year-old daughter. My husband did this because he knows that she's the least likely to finish her dinner.

As my niece Hanna ate dinner, my husband sat hovering over her shoulder, staring down at her plate, tracking the food like a vulture.

Finally, as my husband began to grow impatient with hunger, he turned to the poor kid and asked her, "Are you going to eat that?"

I kicked my husband, the cheap bastard, in the ankle underneath the table.

"What? She's not going to eat it!" My husband looked at me as if he was the victim.

I kicked him again, even harder.

"Ow! Stop that!" he complained.

He's even tried to pull the same crap at dinners with our friends.

If one of our friends is lingering too long over their meal, my husband will attempt to separate them from their food.

"You know people are starving all over the world," he'll say to them.

"To save money he'll forgo ordering."

"I'm just saying it would be a shame to throw it away, is all." Our friend listened to my husband in disbelief, and then shook his head in disgust.

"What are you talking about, throwing my food away?" our friend accused my husband. "I just started eating. Why don't you order something to eat if you're so hungry?"

Needless to say none of our friends will go out to eat with us anymore because of my husband's cheapness. Nowadays when I'm asked out to dinner by a new group of friends, I lie to them and tell them my husband is busy and then I go with them alone. Even worse, I lie to my husband and tell him I'm having a girls' night out. I feel bad about this but I don't feel like I have a choice. If it was up to my husband, we'd never have friends again!

– Susan, Los Angeles CA

23

B.Y.O.T. (BRING YOUR OWN TOPPINGS)

My husband Nick loves adding extra stuff to his food, but he hates paying extra for it. He refuses to fork up the additional cost for toppings when he can just bring cheese slices, avocado or bacon from home, or get them for free. He's always trying to figure out ways to beat the system. I can appreciate his wanting to save money and be thrifty, but his behavior when we go out to eat is just appalling. Unfortunately, we both love to eat out, but for completely different reasons. I love it because I enjoy eating restaurant food. He loves it just because it gets him out of the house.

So, when I tell the waiter I'd like to add cheese to an order, Nick will interrupt. "No, don't add it! I've got her covered."

"Okay," says the waiter as he walks away, not knowing what else to say.

"What do you mean, you've got me covered? I want cheese on my chicken sandwich."

"You want cheese? I'll get you cheese. Don't worry. Nothing's too good for my baby."

So, when they bring out our food, he'll take his butter knife and scrape disgusting blobs of melted, off-colored cheese onto my plate from off the top his nachos. He thinks I'll be happy with these used, rolled-up balls of nacho cheese on my sandwich.

"You keep that plastic-tasting cheese away from my sandwich!" I'll warn him.
It's crazy, but it saves him a dollar, and I can't get him to stop.

Not only will he bring his own toppings and sides but sometimes he'll even take it so far as to ask the server for a discount if he forgoes an item that already comes with the meal. For instance, if he orders a grilled fish dinner that comes with a rice pilaf and vegetable he'll ask something like, "Can I lose the vegetables for $2.50 off the bill? That's how much the sides cost on the menu."

It's so humiliating. The fancier and more expensive the restaurant, the bigger the discount he will try to get and the redder my face will get.

The final straw for me came when we went out to TGI Fridays. My husband ordered a special cheeseburger, "sans" the cheese. He wanted $1.50 off the price of the burger, which was the price on the menu to get extra cheese.

The waiter told him, "Sorry, sir. I can't do that. It's against our policy."
"I'll tell you what, let's split the difference. How 'bout you give me 75 cents off?"

When the burger came, he took two slices of plastic-wrapped, American cheese "product" out of his pocket and added them to the patty.

"Do you have to make a scene every time we go out?" I asked him. "So what? So you saved 75 cents? It's not worth the splitting migraine I'm getting."

"Why should I spend an extra 75 cents on a slice of cheese for my burger when I can bring two slices from home for only 10 cents?" he demanded.

"Because you're buying quality of life and peace of mind for your wife," I said. "Because you care about me and you don't want me to die from stress or embarrassment."

– Penny, Chicago IL

"Who has the audacity to bring slices with them?"

"21st-century morse-code"

THE CODE BREAKER

Occasionally, my husband Mike and I get a collect call from Europe from a "Phil-Goode."

Every time the call comes, we don't accept the charges but I breathe a sigh of relief, because I know my son Tim is fine.

Let me explain:

My husband Mike, cheap bastard that he is, won't let me talk directly to my son on the phone. He says it's too expensive. He doesn't even own a computer, so emailing is even out of the question.

So Mike invented a whole system of communicating with our son for free, using secret code words. I suppose Mike is still entertaining ideas of being some kind of secret agent.

His "scam" works like this:

He has our son call us collect, using different code names for a series of different messages. Then my husband declines to accept the charges for the call and we don't get billed. If Tim's fine, then he'll say his name is "Phil Goode." If Tim is traveling on the weekends, he calls collect as "Seymour Rhodes." "Seymour Rhodes." Can you believe it?

Mike even has an elaborate code worked out for our son to communicate his exact time and date of arrival when he finally decides to stop gallivanting around Europe and needs a ride home from the airport. Tim uses the alphabet to indicate the time he is coming in. For example, if his plane is going to land at 4 o'clock, his name will start with a "D", because "D" is the fourth letter in the alphabet. So he might collect call as David Plane. "D" for 4 o'clock, and plane, because, well...he's coming in on an airplane.

Of course, my crazy husband always declines the collect calls no matter what name my son uses. But I guess the relevant information does get across and we do save money. I'll give him that.

Unfortunately, it doesn't always work out so well. One time my third cousin on my mother's side called collect from jail. The poor guy needed to post bail. Well, my cousin's name is Buster Anderson. My husband thought it was our son calling to inform us that he needed to be picked up at 1:00 am from the local bus station. My unlucky cousin sat in jail for several days while my stupid husband sat up all night waiting in the bus station parking lot.

– Morgan, Detroit MI

DADDY'S LITTLE REMOVER

I think I'm a smart, thrifty shopper. Well, try telling that to my husband. If you ask him he'll tell you I spend too much.

To curb my spending, my husband's devised a devious, sneaky, infuriating (but I must admit, effective) plan. He has secretly hired someone to surreptitiously remove items from my basket as I'm shopping. And guess who he paid to conduct this top-secret operation? Our six-year-old son!

At first, I didn't know what to think. Every time I came home from the store, things were missing from my shopping bags. I thought I was losing my mind. Then I started getting pissed. The main items I went to the store for in the first place would be mysteriously missing from both my bags and from the receipt.

After a while I became suspicious. Unless I had some serious mental problems, something stunk to high heaven. It was a conspiracy.

Then, one time, as I was walking through our local department store, looking for sale items, I noticed that my son kept trying to divert my attention. He wanted me to leave the cart alone for a minute to check out something across the aisle.

At that point, I didn't know why, but I knew my son was the culprit. It wasn't hard to get him to flip and sell out his father. One ice-cream cone and two action figures later, I had him singing like a canary.

My cheap husband was paying our son 50 cents for every item he stole and purged from my shopping cart. Imagine, my husband using my own son against me. I was furious.

I told my son I'd give him $5 if he left Mommy's basket alone forever. We shook on it and then I offered my son a dollar for every one of his father's cigars that he could steal and bring to me for bounty. After all, isn't turnabout fair play?

– Linda, Moorhead MN

"Things were always missing from my shopping bag."

"Risk-free or your money back."

60-DAY MAN

Around our house we call my husband Charlie the "60 Day Man."

He'll purchase a mattress that has a 10-year warranty and keep it for 9 years and 11 months. Then, during the last month of the warranty, he'll return the mattress and get it exchanged for a new one.

He does this when it comes to virtually all the appliances, gadgets and accessories in our lives. He plays the warranty card with vacuum cleaners, washers, dryers, blenders, air conditioners, heaters, DVD players and stereo equipment.

How he is able to keep track of all those deadlines I'll never know. Maybe somewhere hidden in his office he has a secret warranty calendar filled with nothing but expiration dates?

Last January, we had really bad rainstorms. The fallout was that all the homes in our neighborhood, including our own, got flooded. As a result we had to purchase a wet/dry vac to clean the floors.

We shopped around, but a new high-powered wet/dry vac cost more than $500. Renting one, we found, wouldn't be cost-effective either.

Charlie just happened to see an infomercial around that time, which advertised a wet/dry vac for sale with a guaranteed risk-free, 60-day trial period.

He ordered the wet vac and, three days later, used it to clean our home. When we were finished with the vacuum, he actually rented it out to our neighbors to clean their houses.

When the neighbors were done he returned the vac to the company and got his money back. On top of that he had made $300 from our neighbors!

What a freakin' cheap bastard.

– Cindy, Santa Barbara CA

TO-GO, OR NOT TO-GO?

When we have dinner with my sister's family, they all make fun of my husband Todd. They have a cute pet name for my husband. They call him "Mr. To-Go."

"Oh no, it's Mr. To-Go," my brother-in-law will say jokingly as my husband walks in through the front door carrying a large Tupperware container in his hands. My family nicknamed him this because he always brings food home with him when we visit on holidays or drive down for the occasional dinner.

What my family doesn't know is that Todd does the same thing everywhere we go. When we go to the homes of friends, neighbors, or coworkers, there my husband is right before we leave, stealing the leftovers from the kitchen.

Whenever we eat with his family, they're always trying to force us to take leftovers. You'd think I didn't take good care of my husband or that he was all skin and bones the way they try to stock us up with dishes at the door.

"He'll take that to-go."

It can be a little embarrassing at times, but I've come to accept my husband's little quirk and I've never made a big deal out of it. That is, it wasn't a big deal until I brought my husband to a company picnic.

I'd just started working for this new company, and it was my first year attending their annual picnic. I wanted to make a good impression, and I was afraid my husband would embarrass me with his "leftover lifting." However, when we left the house in the morning, I noticed that my husband didn't have his Tupperware with him, for a change. I didn't know why he had left it behind, or whether he forgot it but I figured it was better to let sleeping dogs lie and not bring it up.

We had a great time at the picnic: swimming, playing volleyball, eating barbeque, and socializing with my coworkers.

When we were ready to leave I was thinking I was so proud of my husband for not trying to bring back any food. Then, just as we were literally inches away from the door, my husband stopped a server who was wearing a white apron and taking out the trash.

"Excuse me," my husband said. "Are you throwing any of that food away?

I covered my face, petrified with embarrassment, as the server went to procure several cardboard boxes full of food.

He came back with three boxes total. My husband stacked one on top of the other and then asked me to carry the third one. I shook my head, mortified, and then left the cafeteria area empty handed. I scurried out the door.

A few minutes later, he managed to make his way out the door while balancing the three stacked boxes. He struggled to keep them from falling onto the ground as he looked around, searching for me. Although I was standing right in front of him, he didn't recognize me; I'd put on my sunglasses, thrown a hat onto my head, and wrapped my sweater around my waist like a makeshift skirt. It turned out to be a clever disguise. If my husband didn't recognize me, nobody would.

I grabbed the boxes from him, one at a time, and quickly loaded them into the trunk.

If you can't beat him, join him, right?

– Ana, Daly City CA

"Let me punch those for you."

BUY NONE, GET 1 FREE

When my husband Hugh and I first started dating, he used to take me out to restaurants that use frequent-buyer club cards. The situation in most of these kinds of places is that you buy ten items from the menu, get your card punched for each item, and then get a free item, on the eleventh transaction.

Hugh seemed to have cards for every coffee shop or café in town, but all his cards were filled up with 10 stamps, or 10 novelty shape holes from custom punchers.

At the time I just I figured he had so many cards because he was a bachelor and probably went out to eat a lot.

Little did I know my husband was cheating the system and was just too cheap to pay for his food.

He will actually go into a coffee shop or restaurant and flirt with the cashier to get extra stamps on his card. He's even somehow talked the waitress at one coffee shop near the house into getting him a copy of their custom hole-puncher. That way he could just give himself a free purchase whenever he felt like getting a coffee.

Of course, he never flirted in front of me, but my daughter sold him out and told me all about it. One day, as I was putting away the laundry, I discovered his stash of cards, stamps, and one custom puncher in the back of his sock drawer.

I felt like I should teach him a lesson for being so cheap. I grabbed all of his "free meal gear" and went to the park where I gave his whole collection away to homeless people.

The next day, when he found out what I did, he confronted me.

"How could you throw those away?" he complained.
"Do you realize how much money I've been saving?"

"Don't worry," I told him.
"I'm sure your girlfriend at the coffee shop will give you another puncher."

My husband got quiet and never mentioned another discount club card again.

– Michelle, Berkeley CA

IS THAT COUCH EMPTY?

Remember the good ol' days, when you'd travel out of town and you would crash out on a friend's couch, floor, garage, or even in their hallway? Basically, any place you could lay your head down for the night was fair game.

It was housing on the cheap, which was okay, since we were young and crazy. It was kind of fun. But although I grew up and became an adult, it seems, mentally, my husband never left college.

My husband is 40 years old, we have two kids, and the guy's still couch-surfing every time he takes a trip.

He refuses to pay for a hotel. He'll ambush friends and family a day before he's supposed to fly, asking them to put him up. Of course, by the time he calls them, all the hotels in town are full and his prospective hosts are left without much choice.

He will literally call anyone that either he or I are related to. Forget about the fact that he hasn't seen his third cousin since his sister's wedding when he was 14 years old.

"I'm due for a visit," he'll tell me.
"It's important for families to stay in touch over the years."

What a crock of B.S.!

Forget that he hasn't had any contact whatsoever with his Aunt Barbara in over five years. During that whole time not one phone call, letter, or birthday card changed hands between the two of them, but that didn't stop my husband from calling her up when he had a sales conference in Seattle last spring.

He feels no shame about inconveniencing people to save a couple of lousy bucks.

If my house-crashing husband is looking for a place to stay when he travels, and the well's run dry on family, extended or otherwise, willing to put him up, he'll turn to his friends. He'll turn to old friends from college, from high school even. He'll turn to his Facebook friends, and then he'll turn to a friend of a friend of a Facebook friend, if he has to. He'll catch one of these unsuspecting "missing links" in his social network by surprise and suddenly impose himself on them with his bed-and-breakfast hustle.

"The 40 year old couch surfer"

I hate to say it, but he's like a con artist. He'll show up at the homes of complete strangers and force those people to reminisce about rowdy, intoxicated times with a common friend whom neither has seen since college.

Before we were married, he used to pull these kinds of stunts on our friends whenever we wanted a place to stay and that was okay, I guess. Honestly, the whole house-surfing thing started getting old when we were in our 20s. And now almost 20 years later it's beyond ancient.

One final word of caution: BEWARE! With the "six degrees of separation" rule in effect, my husband could be calling any one of YOU, at any time. Do not, and I repeat, DO NOT invite him into your home. You'd be better off having a parasite over for dinner.

– Michele, Boulder CO

30

TAKING THE CAKE

I know that there are many women out there who think their husbands are tightfisted, but my husband takes the cake when it comes to being a cheap-ass. I mean literally, he takes the extra chunks of cake from the free sampler bar at the grocery store and shoves them into his pocket in a wad of napkins. He may very well be the cheapest man on the planet. No wait, scratch that...the cheapest person, man or woman. I guess it's possible there could be cheaper outer space aliens somewhere in the entire universe, but somehow I doubt it.

I first noticed what a miser my husband was on our first date. To be fair, he took me out to a pretty nice restaurant. The final bill for dinner was around a hundred bucks. So far, so good, right? But then when my stingy husband goes to leave a tip, he only leaves five dollars. On a hundred-dollar bill, he leaves a five-dollar tip. It was humiliating.

We left the restaurant and I told him I forgot my scarf inside. I didn't even own a scarf. I just couldn't live with ripping off this waiter; he had been so nice to us.

He had stood there patiently as my husband treated the menu like it was his own personal pantry.

"Can I get the fish with this chicken sauce?" my frustrating husband asked, in effect rewriting the menu as he went along. The whole time the waiter was polite and kept his cool. "Also can you bring it with yellow rice," my husband kept pushing. "And can you tell them to substitute the house salad for mashed potatoes with gravy? Oh, and can I get some cranberry sauce?"

If I were that waiter I would have punched my husband's lights out. But he had shown incredible restraint.

I went back to our table and left the waiter an additional 15 dollars.

This would be the first of many battles between my husband and me over the tip when we go out to dinner. Whenever we go out to eat, I always insist to my husband that I'll take care of the tip.

"You pay for the meal," I say. "I'll pay for the tip."

But the miserable S.O.B. will pull the same trick I did on our first date and go back into the restaurant to adjust the tip, except he'll take money away that I already left on the table! You can't do that!

But he does. What a psycho.

"That money could be used to pay for parking!" my cheap, cheap husband will say. "You know how much they charge per hour at these downtown garages?" The most horrible event in a chain of disaster dinners and meals of mayhem occurred recently when we went out with our friends. After dinner I left the waitress a pretty nice tip. It was nice enough that she came over to us to say "thank you."

"If I were the waiter I would have punched him."

Then, as she started to clear the table, my husband reached out and took back a ten-dollar bill right from under her. She looked up at him but didn't know what to say. He just turned and left.

"Oh, my God," I apologized. "I can't believe he just did that!"

But I was prepared. I pulled out another ten and handed it to her with a smile.

When we got home, my hubby got into the shower, and I got into his wallet.....taking my ten-dollar bill back so that it will be in MY wallet for the next time we go out to eat and I have to re-tip our server behind my miserly husband's back.

– Mia, Cypress CA

31

RECYCLED POPCORN TUB MAN

When we go to the theater to see a movie these days, it costs a small fortune. Just for two adult tickets it costs over 20 clams. And then you add in the two kids and snacks, and drinks for everyone. You could be looking at 50 dollars or more just to check out a flick!

Well, my husband's taken a stand against the motion-picture industry. He refuses under any circumstances to pay for popcorn. He considers it a sin.

"Six dollars," he'll complain.
"That's highway robbery! There's no way I'm paying that."

"He started soliciting people leaving the theaters."

"Fine," I'll tell him. "So don't have popcorn."

"But I like popcorn," he'll whine.

There was nothing I could do or say to make him happy.
He wanted to "have his popcorn and eat it too."

And then one day my husband figured out a way to make his popcorn pipe dream a reality.

The large chain movie theaters try to up-sell their patrons on plus-sized drinks and snacks by offering free refills on the largest cups and buckets. But no one can polish off an entire extra large bucket of popcorn during the course of one movie, even if they're sharing the popcorn with their entire family. It just can't be done since those things are so huge!

So, essentially free refills on popcorn and soda at the movies are all a big scam. That is, it was a scam until my scammer husband figured out how to out-scam the scammers.

He started to solicit people leaving the movie theaters for their empty popcorn containers. Then he would bring the empty containers up to the counter and request a free refill. A simple plan, if not a sanitary one.

My disgusting, stingy husband will even dig through the trash at the movies, scavenging for empty popcorn buckets.

"That's so gross," I've complained to him.

I got a huge kick the last time we went to the movies together. As usual, he brought a large empty popcorn bucket from a previous visit up to the concession stand and asked for a free refill. This time, however, the cashier wasn't buying it.

"Um... sir... we changed the design of our popcorn container over a month ago. Where did you find this bucket?"

I started to break into hysterical laughter as my husband gave me the evil eye. He was paralyzed. He didn't have a contingency plan for this type of situation. I did... I tried a radical new approach to acquiring popcorn at the movies... I paid for it.

Since then, whenever I go out with my husband to the movies,
I'm in charge of the snacks.

– Jennifer, Los Angeles CA

32

THE GUY THAT KEEPS
ON GIFTING

I can't remember the last time my husband actually purchased a gift for someone. He is the world's best, or I should say worst, re-gifter.

I used to get upset about it but then I realized, "Why fight it?" I could try to keep arguing with him and lose since I can't ever get him to admit he's doing anything wrong. Or I can sit back and watch and let him do his cheapskate thing while I gain entertainment value out of his shenanigans.

It can actually be sort of fascinating to watch the great re-gifter in action. His antics go beyond any normal measure of what's considered a cheap thing to do and border on some sort of demented brilliance.

His greatest weapon in his re-gifting arsenal is his world-view. He's the kind of guy that believes he already has everything he needs in his life and therefore doesn't need anything new. Since he never wants presents that anyone gives him, he feels justified in re-gifting his presents and circulating them back into the gift pool, under false pretenses.

My "gift grifter" husband gets away with it by only unwrapping a tiny corner of any present he receives. He neatly creates a window just big enough to see what's inside and then thanks the person. Later, he folds the wrapping paper closed again and then prepares to re-gift.

He has an entire system for keeping track of presents he gets. He's very well organized for a psychotic. After he gets a gift, he labels it with a sticky note that indicates what the item is and when it was given to him. The sticky notes are color coded. Different hues are used to indicate whether the present came from a family member, friend, co-worker or stranger. That way, he's able to avoid re-gifting it back to the person who gave it to him in the first place.

"The re-gifter meets his match."

With few exceptions, he doesn't keep any presents ever given to him. All gifts immediately go into The Gift Relocation Program.

He keeps his gifts stored in large plastic containers in our garage until a birthday, wedding or other gift-giving event comes along.

This system served him well until just recently, when he, the expert re-gifter, crossed paths with his arch nemesis– the new receptionist at his office, also known as "the expert re-packager." What the re-packager does is take the boxes she gets gifts in and reuses them with other gifts inside. It can be kind of annoying when you unwrap a present but you don't actually get what the box leads you to believe is inside.

I guess on the other hand though, it can be kind of a good thing, if you hate the item that the box originally came in. When you discover that there's a different present inside it's like getting a second chance at a good gift.

This past Christmas, the re-packager gave my husband a gift packed it in a box that originally had a chenille blanket in it.

We didn't find out about the re-packaging job until a few days later when my mother was opening her gift from my husband. Instead of the beautiful blanket that was featured in the photo on the box, she was perplexed to be holding a golf shirt with my husband's initials embroidered on the collar.

– Mary, Nashville TN

33

MOVIE HOPPER

So you think your husband is cheap? Well, my spouse is the Chief of Cheap, the Prince of Penny Pinching.

He flat out refuses to pay $12 for a movie at our local theater.

"When we first started dating, you know how much it cost us? Two bucks! That's it! And popcorn was 50 cents!"

I wouldn't mind so much if he were just complaining about it to me; I've gotten really good at tuning him out. But.....he tells the ticket-taker at the theater.

I'll hang my head in embarrassment as my husband annoys the bored teenager who takes our tickets and hands us back the stubs. "Second theater on the right. Enjoy the show. Next."

The worst part is that my husband will fork over the money for two tickets and then demand we sneak into another movie afterwards to get our money's worth. He doesn't see anything wrong with it though. For him, the movie theater is like an all-you-can-eat buffet full of new releases. I think he might have a real serious problem.

On Thursday night after work, my husband will sit down and check the movie listings for the weekend. He'll map out an entire schedule based around the sequence of different movies he wants to see, their running times and what time they start. Once a month on a Saturday, first thing in the morning when the multiplexes open, my husband is there, first in line. He'll pay the discounted matinee price of $7 and then just stay there the entire day watching movies! From 11 a.m. until midnight he'll stay at the theater!

One Saturday, when his scheduling skills were off, I made the mistake of going with him, because there happened to be two movies playing that I wanted to see. My husband's so-called "schedule" had us hanging around for an hour and a half between movies. He had us lay low in our seats, like fugitives. Later he even wanted me to hide out in the ladies room for 45 minutes. I said, "There's no way I'm going to hole up in a dirty bathroom stall so you can save five dollars!"

After a moment of scheming, I told him, "I'll make you a deal. I'll pay you five dollars right now if you take me home!"

I mentioned my husband won't buy snacks? That's not the worst of it. He brings his own snacks. That sounds harmless, right? Wrong. He doesn't make smart, sensible choices with his movie theater cuisine. I mean, I could understand if he wanted to bring a candy bar from home, but re-heated chicken wings? It can be so, so humiliating. Like, when we went to see *Lord of the Rings*, my husband smuggled in a Tupperware container full of salmon cutlet leftovers under his shirt.

"All-you-can-eat buffet full of new releases"

The whole theater was packed that night, and every single person in there could smell my husband's "snack." "Let all those suckers buy overpriced snacks at the concession stand. I'm eating my leftovers. End of story."

"Excuse me, sir, but do you have to eat that smelly fish right now? The smell of that is...overpowering, I'm a vegetarian and I feel very nauseous right now," the lady next to him said. Talk about embarrassing.

I got up and left the theater. I can wait five months and see it on DVD!

– Kirsten, Cleveland OH

"He's constantly timing his cell phone calls."

34

THE MINUTEMAN

During the American Revolution there were these soldiers called minutemen. They were called minutemen because of their readiness to respond to threats and go into battle.

My husband is a "minute man" too. But a different sort altogether. The only threat that he's ready to respond to is the threat of a large cell phone bill.

He's constantly timing his cell phone calls to make sure he doesn't go over his allotted minutes. Believe me, there's nothing revolutionary about it.

My husband's such a "wolf in cheap's clothing," he actually refuses to accept phone calls during the day. He's terrified of using his "anytime" minutes. When he does take calls, he carefully watches the counter and makes sure that he's off the phone in less than 60 seconds. He'll usually extricate himself from a call by the 55-second mark. If a person keeps talking after about 55 seconds, my husband will hang up on them. Later he'll say he lost the call.

My husband's so bad, he'll already start planning his escape at the very beginning of the phone call. He'll plant seeds for later, from the get-go, by lying to the person on the other end and telling them he's having signal problems.

He even pulls this crap on important calls, like the doctor's office or our daughter's teacher. He'll even do it to his poor, old grandmother, who is hard of hearing. Most of the time, she doesn't even realize that he's hung up the phone. She's still talking, and he's off the phone, flipping channels with the remote.

Oddly enough, he never seems to have any of these connection problems during off-peak hours and weekends when minutes are free.

Our family and friends have caught on to him though. This past Christmas, since he's been "complaining" so much about his phone dropping so many calls, everyone we know chipped in and bought him a new cell phone.

– Joyce, Atlanta GA

→**35**

MANY HAPPY RETURNS

My wedding day was such an exciting time for me that I completely overlooked the fact that I was getting married to a miser.

I knew from dating him that Greg could be a tightwad. But I never expected him to skimp on his own tuxedo, or his own wedding!

When we got to the reception after the wedding ceremony, I noticed my husband had some duct tape stuck to the bottom of his shoe. I looked closer and there was yet another piece of duct tape sticking out from under his right pants leg.

I confronted him, and he admitted that he intended to return the tuxedo to the store after the wedding. Not only had he left the tags on his tux but, instead of getting a tailor to fit the suit to his body, he had adjusted the hemline himself with duct tape, on the inside of his pants legs! He had even put tape on the soles and heels of his shoes to avoid scuffing them. He actually planned to return his shoes too!

I felt like I had just discovered a terrible secret about my new husband, a frightening skeleton in the closet.

And then my husband actually had the nerve to suggest that we return my wedding dress too to save money! My wedding dress!

Considering how freaking cheap he is, I actually entertained the notion for a second. Maybe I would return the wedding dress to the store...and then leave his cheap ass.

Instead I let him off with a warning. I said, "If you ever again suggest to me that I return my wedding dress, we're getting a divorce." That's a nice way to start the first day of a marriage, but what could I do? There had to be some ground rules to our life together.

Besides, if he keeps this crap up, I might need to wear the dress again...when I marry someone else.

– Jessica, Boston MA

"I confronted him and
he admitted his intentions."

"He researches policies on all purchases."

PROFESSIONAL PRICE ADJUSTER

My husband is a PPA: Professional Price Adjuster. He's the guy who is always hustling to get the lowest possible price on a product.

Though you could argue my husband is crazy, he's also a very organized PPA. He keeps a file folder with all the receipts he ever gets. He literally has one folder for each day of the month. Before he makes a purchase at any store, my husband researches that store's policy on price adjustments. If the product he purchases goes on sale within 14 to 30 days from the time he purchases it, he wants a refund on the difference.

Lots of people do this with high-end items like cameras or computers. If a camera goes on sale from $300 to $250, it's reasonable to ask for a $50 rebate. My husband takes price adjustments to an entirely different place however. He wants price adjustments on everything he buys, from toothpaste to furniture.

When he bought a power tool from a store that didn't offer price adjustments, he never even took it out of the box. He kept calling the store every week to see if it had gone on sale. Finally, 30 days later, he dragged me down to the store and had me buy the same tool at the sale price while he went to customer service to return the one he never opened.

When I finally took the time to calculate the amount of money my husband saves versus the amount he spends on overhead, I came to a troubling conclusion.

We live out on a farm that is at least half an hour away from the nearest town. The cost of the gas that my husband burns to get his price adjustments, let alone the money he spends each month on manila folders, worked out so that sometimes we just break even. Other times we lose money!

Recently I overheard our 14-year-old daughter on the phone calling a store to check to see if her new shoes were on sale yet.

"I know you have a 30-day policy," my daughter haggled, "but it's only been 31 days. Can I still get the price adjustment, please?"

Great! Not only is my husband a cheapskate, but he's turned my daughter into one too. She even has her own little file folder.

– Dorine, Sonoma CA

START ME UP

My husband Chris is such a cheap you-know-what, he'd rather continuously jumpstart our car rather than buying a new battery.

Granted, I'm not talking about Chris's everyday car. It's the first car he ever owned from back when he was in high school and he only uses it occasionally. Nevertheless, when he does use that car, it's a nightmare. It's so embarrassing to have to ask for a jump every single time we go anywhere.

My husband tries to hide his cheap secret from people, by alternating who he asks for a jump. If he's already gotten a jump that month from his brother, he'll ask his best friend, and after that his mother...and then...the next-door neighbor. He doesn't want anyone to know that he actually does this kind of thing all the time.

Sometimes I wonder if he enjoys having people see him working under the hood, as if it shows off his manliness or something. But then I think, "No...he's just cheap."

When my parents came to visit for the holidays he offered them our good car so they didn't have to deal with the jumping situation. He used his old car but didn't get a new battery.

You'd think if you only have one car to use and it doesn't have a battery, you'd just bite the bullet and buy the new battery. My husband doesn't think like that.

So there we were in the dead of winter, sitting in the freezing car on the side of the road, waiting, hoping, praying that some kind stranger would come along and stop to share some juice. Eventually, when no one came, my husband had to walk to a payphone and call my parents to come give us a jump. How humiliating!

On Christmas morning, Chris went to pick up one his presents that was gift wrapped under the tree. It was heavier than he expected it to be for its size and he strained his back. Inside was a brand-new car battery from my parents.

Not only is my husband cheap, but he's also lazy! It's been three months since the holidays and he still hasn't put the new battery in the car yet.

If he doesn't get a grip on the situation soon, he's going to have a different kind of battery to worry about...assault and battery!

– Courtney, Colorado Springs CO

"It's so embarrassing to have to ask for a jump every single time we go anywhere."

"I saved myself $15 a day on parking."

38

LONG-TERM PARKING, SHORT-TERM PRICING

Because my husband works for a large corporation as one of their field managers, he has to travel to other cities about once or twice a month. Ever since I was late to pick him from the airport one time, several years ago, he insists on driving himself.

It was no big deal when my husband's company used to reimburse him for the $20 a day he'd spend on airport parking. Recently however, with the bad state of the economy, the company has stopped footing the bill for its employees' parking expenses.

Rather than pay the $20 per day himself for parking like a normal person would do, he's devised a clever way to beat the system, and get discounted parking.

Instead of using the actual airport parking lot, he'll go to a service station a couple of blocks away. When he gets there, he'll ask for a $12.99 oil change special or some other kind of inexpensive servicing. Then he'll tell the service station attendant that he'll be back to pick up his car in a few days.

They usually let him get away with it and, instead of paying $60 for parking while he's gone on a three-day trip, he ends up only paying $12.99 plus tax!

I wouldn't be surprised if his car has over 10 oil changes in a year.

But last month, he finally got his comeuppance. After he finally returned from a trip to Minneapolis, where he'd gotten snowed in for two extra days, he went to pick up his car at the service station, but it was nowhere to be found. He inquired about it, frantically worried that it had been stolen.

"Oh, no, sir. It's fine," the friendly service manager told him. "We assumed you got held up, so we figured we'd be nice and drive it to the long-term parking structure down the street. It's much safer there anyway."

Now, he finally accepts my offers for rides to the airport. No oil change required!

– Rebecca, Salt Lake City UT

→39

LOST & FOUND AND FOUND

I hear horror stories of all these women complaining about how cheap their husbands are. Well, no offense, ladies, but your men have nothing on my miser. Are you ready for this? My husband does his shopping at the "Lost and Found."

No, the "Lost and Found" is not the name of some new, high-end, suburban, clothing store in competition with The Gap and other trendy stores at the shopping mall. Nor is the "Lost and Found" a clever name for a thrift or used, vintage-clothing store. Whenever my cheap husband needs to buy clothes or accessories, instead of paying for these items, he acquires them from the lost-and-found bins at department stores, libraries, and malls.

It all started a few months ago when my husband left his jacket at the gym. The busy trainer behind the front desk gave him free range to search through an entire lost-and-found closet. I was double-parked at the curb out front of the fitness center. My husband was supposed to be "just running in" to pick up his coat.

Twenty minutes later, after trying unsuccessfully several times to reach my husband by cell phone, I was considering leaving him behind. Just as I was about to pull out of the parking lot, he came jogging through the gym's glass doors wearing his missing jacket. In addition, hoisted over his shoulder was a backpack that he hadn't brought in with him.

He jumped into the passenger seat and slammed the front door closed.

"Drive!" he demanded urgently before even buckling his seat belt.

"What's going on?" I asked him. "What's with the backpack?"

"It was in the free box."

"Free box?" I said. "I thought it was a lost-and-found?"

"Free box, lost-and-found. Same difference."

> "Free box, lost-and-found.
> Same difference."

Since that incident, and despite my objections, my husband has become quite the lost-and-found treasure hunter.

Whenever he or my kids need anything, be it scarves, gloves, hats, sweaters, or sunglasses, rather than shopping like a normal person, he will first check at the nearest department store, library, hotel, or movie theater and pretend to have lost his desired item. He'll go shopping for anything desirable in the lost-and-found. It's ridiculous and outright criminal.

Most places don't let my husband just dig around and look for his own item, but when they do, that's what he considers a "big score." When they let him loose, he goes on a "free stuff free-for-all." If the employees at a store won't grant my husband carte-blanche, unfettered access to the lost-and-found bin, then he has a contingency plan. He comes prepared with lies.

Recently on our fifth wedding anniversary, my husband gave me this really ornate, glamorous necklace. With that, he almost bought his way into another year of happy marriage. But then I had to wonder, "Did my doting husband scrounge for months to make this thoughtful gift happen? Or did he just pocket someone else's left-behind anniversary gift?" Knowing how my husband is, I'm guessing that right now, there's probably some soon-to-be-single, brow-beaten man searching in vain through the lost-and-found bin at Nordstrom for his own missing present to his wife.

If there's any man alive that could potentially kill two marriages with one stone, it's my hubby.

– Elaine, Las Vegas NV

"To save money he stopped
flushing the toilet."

MELLOW YELLOW

My husband is so cheap that he's actually begun to endanger our lives. Seriously, don't get my wrong. I don't mind the coupon clipping, the bargain chasing, or the fact that he rarely takes me out to dinner. I don't even mind the finagling and the haggling my husband engages in when we go appliance shopping. All of the above I can live with, and in some cases, even appreciate.

Finally though, he crossed the line and I had to put my foot down when he put the health of our family at risk.

To save money on our water bill, my husband recently stopped flushing the toilet. He only flushes on every third pee– leaving the bowl filled with his disgusting, festering urine, two thirds of the time, on every "off pee." He claims to have devised a mathematical formula whereby only flushing every third pee, we'd save eight percent every month on our water bill. How he arrived at these exact figures I can't really say. I'm a little suspicious since he's not all that talented at doing math. He can't even do long division without a calculator.

At first I chalked this habit of his up to laziness. I mean, I had brothers growing up. I know that it's in men's nature to be pigs.

I finally complained to him about "the pee" a few weeks ago. He shrugged and mumbled some half-assed acknowledgement of my concerns. Later that day I went to use the bathroom, and lo and behold, the pee's still there!

It was starting to become a real health concern. Our bathroom was like a public restroom in a Calcutta bus station! I tried everything to get him to stop. I downloaded articles and clippings from the Internet and tacked them onto the bulletin board in his home office. Then I started leaving critical and abrasive post-it notes stuck to his computer monitor.

For example, on one post-it note I left him, I wrote, "You might not be flushing your urine, but you ARE flushing our marriage down the toilet!"

Despite my half-serious threats, my husband could not be deterred. "You'd rather we flush away our money?" he asked, as he held my latest post-it note, crumpled into a yellow ball in his fist.

It got to the point where I could no longer take it. I decided that what my husband needed was an intervention. I ambushed him when he had a doctor's appointment for his bi-annual check-up. I had called in advance and left a message with our doctor about our little "pee-pee" situation. Apparently, when the doctor saw my husband, he really chewed him a new one as he mercilessly hammered away at his irresponsibility.

As a compromise, we installed a toilet-tank water saver. Now, he's happy because we're saving Dead Presidents and I'm happy because we're not dead from a bathroom-borne bubonic plague.

- Rosemary, San Jose CA

STAMPS OF DISAPPROVAL

As a society, we spend so much money on modern forms of communication that, compared to the cost of cell phones and Internet access (and all the accessories that come with them) the few cents a postage stamp costs are .....well, just that... ..a few pennies. Nevertheless, my husband Ernie will commit mail fraud and risk incarceration in a federal prison, in order to save 43 cents.

If you mail a letter that's lacking the proper postage amount, rather than throw your mail away the post office will just send it back to you. Your letter will be marked "return to sender" and "undeliverable due to insufficient postage" and will wind up back in your mailbox.

Ernie has a trick to save money and beat the system though. What he does is write the address of the person he intends to send the letter to in the "from" area (upper left-hand corner), as if that person was the sender. That way, when the post office takes his unmetered and unstamped letter and tries to "Return to Sender," they're actually sending it where my husband wanted it to go! In essence, my husband makes the intended recipients of his mail send letters to themselves while he gets a stamp-free joyride! That is so sneaky and devious, it makes me suspicious about the whole marriage.

The worst, and most embarrassing, parts of my husband's cheapskate postal scam are the people who he's sending the letters to. He doesn't even let them in on his plan, until afterwards. He does this to his family, friends, and coworkers. He'll even sink so low as to use his trick and R.S.V.P. "sans stamps" to a wedding.

This past Mother's Day, I got a confused call from my mother-in-law. She wanted to know why a piece of mail addressed as being from her was sent to her house. She said her name and address were in the left-hand corner of the envelope, as well as in "addressee" area, but that it wasn't her handwriting.

"He'll commit mail fraud to save a few pennies."

"Why would I send a card to myself on Mother's Day?" she demanded. "Besides," she continued, "if I were mailing something, I would have used stamps!"

I couldn't believe my deadbeat husband had pulled this trick on his own mother! And, here I was, the one who had to deal with all the fallout. I had to explain to her that her son was so cheap, he'd resorted to breaking the law to save a couple of dimes.

I could hear the sadness in her voice.

"Do you need to borrow some money?" she asked me.
"Are you two having financial troubles?"

"No," I snapped, defensively, and then caught myself.
"We're fine. Everything's fine."

She paused for a moment as she processed the situation, then she completely caught me off guard with her next remark.

"Then let him know that, for his birthday next month, he can put a 20-dollar bill into a card and send it to himself from me."

Jennifer, Portland OR

42

GAS MARATHON MAN

With the price of gas going through the roof whenever OPEC feels like flexing their muscles, it's reasonable to seek and be savvy for the best gas bargains, but my husband Joe does this to a fault. To a certain extent it saves us money, but the lengths he goes to on his quest for value are ultimately too much.

Joe knows by heart the cheapest gas station, not just in our neighborhood or town, but in the entire county. He'll spend nearly an hour every day conducting online research on gas station locations. He wants to stay informed with the most up-to-date, minute-by-minute gas prices. To say my husband is an obsessive-compulsive when it comes to finding the best gas prices would be like pointing out that that the ocean is wet or that the Pope is Catholic. It's an understatement. He takes his gas-station mania to the point where it's a crippling social disorder.

He recently found out that one local membership-required discount store's gas station had the cheapest gas in our entire county. But instead of forking over the money for the membership, my husband wanted to borrow his friend's card.

Sure, okay, cheap gas, plus a free ride on a membership card. Nothing wrong with that, right? He's just saving money. Okay, but here's the problem. He had to drive 15 minutes in the wrong direction to get the card and then another 45 minutes to the store, which is about a half hour away from the house already.

Add that to the fact that he drives a giant SUV and gets less than 10 miles to the gallon, and his $1.46 saving on 12 gallons of gas cost him over $5 in gas spent on the trip,

I said to him, "Dear…are you going to drive over to Kenny's house and then all the way to that store, every time you need a fill-up?"

Poor stupid bastard just didn't get the logic behind what I was saying.
You can't spend a quarter to save a nickel.

It's not possible that we could be saving any money with the amount of gas my husband guzzles while searching for cheap gas. Maybe, if I could somehow harness the energy my husband puts into finding cheap gas to make some sort of alternative fuel out of the time he wastes each week, then we'd be on Easy Street.

– Rekha, Sacramento CA

"He drives an SUV, but thinks
he's saving on gas."

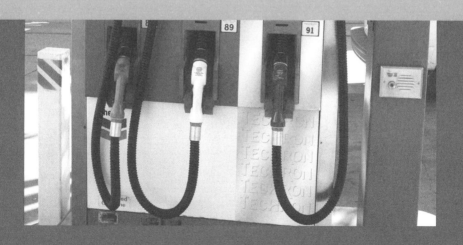

43

SANTA CLAUS IS COMING, JUST NOT WHEN YOU THINK

Sometimes when you're a parent, telling a little white lie can be alright, even encouraged. For example, it's okay when you fib to your children and tell them that the Easter Bunny is real. Society deems that fabrication acceptable despite the fact that you're populating your children's world-views and perceptions of reality with giant egg-laying rabbits.

My husband Sam takes these little innocent white lies and turns them into an intricate spider web of white lies. He thinks that since the whole story of Santa Claus is make-believe to begin with, he can tell more lies and add to the story in any way, anytime he sees fit. The worst part is he'll use our children's' naïve belief in old Saint Nick to cover up his own cheapness!

My cheap husband refuses to buy any presents before Christmas because the best deals come after Christmas. Buying full-price retail merchandise is for "suckers," Sam always says.

Every year he lies to our children, and every year as they get older, they become more skeptical of his lies. This last year he tried to sell them on the B.S. line that because of "overpopulation and traffic," Santa can't get to every house on Christmas Eve.

"I got an email from Santa," my husband told our kids, "he's not going to make it until Friday."

In previous years the kids had believed him hook, line and sinker, no matter how ridiculous the excuse he made for Santa Claus was.

I recall one year when he claimed that "Santa's sled is in the shop."

Another year he told them that one of Santa's reindeer was sick and Santa had to stay home and nurse "Blitzen" back to health.

He might as well have told our kids,
"Santa got pulled over for speeding and was arrested with a DWI."

Can you believe the nerve of my husband?

On Christmas day he tried to keep the kids busy with cartoons and board games so that they wouldn't ask to play with the neighbor's kids. He didn't want them to find out that their friends already got presents. What Sam didn't think through was that, by the age of seven, a little girl has already been using telephones and gabbing with her little friends for about five years. My husband almost got

"Christmas always comes late at our house."

busted when little Judy Davidson called up our Cindy and told her that "Santa" had already visited her house. When my daughter got off the phone, she had some uncomfortable questions for my husband.

"But I don't understand," she complained. "Judy lives right across the street. Why would Santa go to her house but not ours?"

To my daughter's credit, she smelled a rat. She was smart enough now to realize that Santa's probably not real, and that even if he is real he would inevitably disappoint her. That's the lesson my husband taught our children this Christmas. What a father!

– Mary, San Diego CA

44

IT'S YOUR BIRTHDAY

A person's birthday is supposed to be special. If time and work afford the opportunity, most people like to spend their birthdays in a relaxing way. Maybe they like to treat themselves to a nice meal in a fancy restaurant or take in a good movie.

My husband ruins birthdays with his cheap ways. If my husband's birthday falls on a weekday he will take the day off from work. Every year his birthday ritual is the same. From morning to night he will go from restaurant to restaurant getting free meals and desserts for his birthday. My husband has this compendium of every single restaurant, café, and bar in this area that offers free food to people on their birthdays.

It doesn't matter that on his birthday this year, I made him breakfast in bed. He wouldn't even touch it.

"Put the plates in the fridge," my husband said. "I'll eat it later."

"Why would you do that?" I asked him. "After all the trouble I went to?"

"Why waste a free meal?" he said. "Let's go to IHOP and cash in."

On my husband's birthday he will eat anywhere from 6 to 10 meals over the course of an entire day. And that's not even including free appetizers, cakes, or beers. The last straw came this year on my birthday. My husband said he was going to take me out to a nice restaurant. When we instead pulled up to one of the loud, flashy franchise restaurants that I knew was at the top of his birthday list, I refused to get out of the car.

I for one find the whole birthday song and dance at a restaurant to be beyond humiliating. And this was T.G.I.F's, the place where all the waiters clap! There was no way I was going to subject myself to that level of embarrassment. I knew then there was no way I could win with my husband. He'd never agree to pay full price at a restaurant when we could be getting a free meal somewhere else.

"Let's just go to the grocery store and make dinner at home," I told him.

"But we came all this way!" he pushed. "Why not just get your free meal, and if you don't like it, we'll go somewhere else that also has free meals?"

"It's my birthday," I snapped at him. "I want to eat at home. Take me home."

I was upset but I started to calm down once we got to the supermarket. The whole ride I was afraid he was going to try to pull a fast one and trick me into going to another free restaurant. On the ride home, for instance, he started to turn in an unusual direction until I called him out. He claimed he was just taking the scenic route. Yeah, right.

"There's a free meal waiting for you."

If I was going to have a good time and avoid dying of a stress-induced stroke, I had to take control of my own birthday. I had to strip him of his power and authority to spring any birthday surprises on me. In effect I suspended his "surprise license." "You're banned from surprises," I told him. "Don't even think about trying to throw me a surprise party at Chili's."

Well, banned or not, my husband still managed to get me with one final birthday surprise. When we were at the register checking out, he actually asked the cashier if we could have the groceries for free since it was my birthday.

I hung my head in shame. Some birthday present.

– Vanessa, New Orleans LA

"What else do you think you
could smuggle in?"

BYOB

My husband Billy makes a decent living and he treats me right, but sometimes he can just be such a "cheapster."

Every time my husband goes out to a restaurant, he smuggles in wine from home.

For instance, on our first wedding anniversary, we were on our way to go out to eat when he suddenly pulled into a grocery store.

"What are you doing?" I asked him, as he looked for a parking spot.
"Where are we going?"

"I'm going to pick out a bottle of wine," he said casually.

"We're on our way to a restaurant," I protested.
"I don't think you're allowed to do that."

"So what?" he said. "Why should I pay $50 at the restaurant when I can get the same exact thing here for 15 bucks?"

When we got to the restaurant, Billy tried to sneak the wine out of his coat and onto the table but got busted by the waiter, who told my husband that the restaurant had a "no outside food or beverages, no exceptions" policy. My husband appealed to him with an outright lie, telling the waiter that we had drunk this specific brand of wine on our very first date.

We hadn't even had wine on our first date– it was tequila shots!

Finally the waiter gave into Billy but not until my husband had made a scene and embarrassed us in front of the entire restaurant. If he hadn't gotten me a gorgeous tennis bracelet for our anniversary, I might have been really upset.

We went out to a different restaurant less than a month later and Billy got busted again for trying to smuggle a bottle of wine in under his trench coat. He tried to use the same line on the waitress, about how it was our anniversary and how the wine had sentimental value to him.

Once again, the waitress caved in and let it go, only after he had made a big to-do about it. When she left, I told my husband, "With all the money you're saving with your cash-saving antics, there'd better be another gift under that trench coat!"

– Summer, Philadelphia PA

FOREVER YOUNG

My husband is so cheap he'll make my kids pretend to be younger than they are to get discounted admission at places like movie theaters, theme parks, and museums.

One time, when we first started dating, he even tried to get a student discount for himself at the movies. He was 34 years old at the time– old enough and established enough to make a decent living! He told the cashier he was a graduate student at the local university. She let him in without even asking to see his I.D.

Now we're married with four boys who are 4, 13, 15 and 16 years old. We live right near a local buffet restaurant in town where kids under the age of 12 eat free. Instead of paying 40 dollars for the entire meal, he ends up paying $10 plus tax and tip. The worst part is that it has to be psychologically damaging to our children. He insists that my oldest son slouch so that he appears to be younger and shorter. The thing is my oldest son is tall and big for his age already, so it's a hard sell. Every time he does it I just feel so embarrassed for the poor kid.

Our two oldest sons are so tired of pretending that they hardly even go out to eat with us anymore. Most of the time they'd rather just stay home and eat leftovers. Imagine that– kids who'd prefer two-day-old tuna casserole to a restaurant meal!

This last summer we took the kids to a theme park where they had discounted prices for kids 12 and under. The cashier took one look at my son's old 6th grade ID, and shook his head. "This can't be you," the cashier said skeptically, looking carefully back and forth between my son and the picture on the card. "Yes, well, he gained a lot of weight just in the past few months," my husband tried to intervene.

I gestured to my other sons, and the rest of us got into a different line. I bought our tickets on the quick and we made our way into the park. I feel really bad for leaving my eldest son behind to deal with my husband, but on the other hand, at least I was able to save three of them.

"You look much younger in this picture."

As crazy as it sounds, part of me wants my boys to hurry up and grow up so I don't have to go through all of this nonsense! I just hope that they don't turn out to be cheap like their father.

They're starting to catch on and deal with it in their own way though– exacting their revenge on their dad in some interesting ways.

For instance, the last time my husband asked them to look younger, they were standing in line behind him at the movie theater as he purchased the tickets. When he turned to hand them their "child" tickets, they all had their thumbs in their mouths.

He was so humiliated by their "childish" behavior that he never requested that they act younger again.

– Sara, Chicago IL

"This is the reason why you never
see the butcher."

HOW MUCH IS THAT T-BONE WITHOUT THE BONE?

My husband is a physician and owns a successful practice. You'd think with his comfortable income level that he wouldn't act like a tightwad? But you'd be wrong to think that.

He shops at a major chain grocer and has a strange strategy for saving money. When he goes to purchase meat at the deli counter, he has them remove all the bones first so that he doesn't have to pay for any of the extra weight. He tells the butcher or counter attendant that he gets the meat for an elderly neighbor that can't deal with the bones. They'll do it for my husband, even though it takes about 10 minutes to strip the bones off and it holds up the line. I guarantee whenever someone from behind the counter sees my husband coming, they run and hide in the back until he's gone.

When I get to the store they even ask me if I want the bone removed because they recognize me as his wife. How horrifying. Of course, anytime they ask, I tell them "no, thanks."

Recently, we went to the market and I gave my husband a public piece of my mind as the butcher was preparing meat to my husband's specs.

"Can you just get a normal piece of meat, like a normal person?" I asked him and pointed to the line behind us.

"Why should I pay for the part of the T-bone I'm not going to eat?" he complained. "The 'T' is all just dead weight."

"By that logic," I countered, "you should peel an orange before you buy it, because you don't want to pay for the part you won't eat."

"That's not a bad idea," he said, and dropped the subject.

I instantly regretted opening my mouth and giving him more bright ideas.

– Tina, Santa Monica CA

METER MADNESS

My husband makes over six figures a year in real estate and the stock market, but you'd never know it by the way he pinches all those pennies he earns.

My husband refuses to pay full price for parking. Whenever we go out and he's driving, I know enough to insist that we leave at least an hour in advance, since he will literally circle around a city block until he finds a metered parking spot with time left on the meter. He just won't cough up the quarters unless he's getting some kind of a break. Sometimes he'll spend a half hour waiting for a car to leave a spot with an hour left on the parking meter.

His logic is that people always leave before their time is up. My husband doesn't mind playing the waiting game. Never mind that he spends more money on gas driving around than he saves on parking.

"What's the point?" I've asked him. "Just pay the meter already!"

If there are only parking garages available in the area where we want to go out, my husband will often park blocks and blocks away from our destination if it means he gets free parking. Recently we went out to eat with some friends, and being such a stingy stickler, he refused to pay the valet. Instead, he dropped me off while he drove around to find a spot. I went into the restaurant and soon found myself in the uncomfortable position of trying to explain why my husband was 30 minutes late for the meal.

"Why can't he find a spot?" one of my friends asked me. "There's a parking lot right across the street."

What could I say? I was too embarrassed to tell them my husband's too miserly to pay for parking. For a second, I thought about lying to our friends and telling them that my husband was having an affair just so that I wouldn't have to admit the shameful truth. How sad is that?

– Shelly, Oakland CA

"He'll spend hours looking
for the right spot."

"What is the point of buying stuff when it's in the office."

COMPANY PILFERER

There is an endless amount of office supplies at our house that my husband Nick steals from work. I'm pretty sure we could open up our own office-supply store with the stolen goods.

My husband works for a big corporate giant that attends trade shows around the world. At these trade shows Nick's company sets up a booth and gives away promotional free stuff like pens, pencils, notepads, and shirts with the company's logo on it. My husband is supposed to be giving all of this material away to potential clients. Half the time, he's just pocketing the crap and bringing it home.

It's bad enough that my cheap husband won't buy our kids new back-to-school supplies when it comes to stationery. The worst part, however, is that he wants our kids to wear the oversized corporate embroidered shirts that he gets from the trade shows. My husband just doesn't see the point in buying the kids new clothes if he can get them free stuff. Meanwhile, our kids get ostracized and teased at school for the way they're dressed when all of the other kids are wearing the latest fashions and name brands.

One year my husband was busy working a trade show right before Christmas. On Christmas day, our oldest son opened up his gift from his dad. "Wow, Dad," our son said, sarcastically shaking his head. "You really shouldn't have. I mean...really."

I was about to chastise our son for taking a fresh tone with his father until I saw the gift he had received. My son had pulled a company sweater out of the box.

I couldn't blame him for being disappointed. If Nick had tried to give me a free present for Christmas, that would have been the end of our marriage, kids or not.

My son was disappointed, but I pulled him aside and we had a little talk, after which he was fine. By the way, you'll never guess what my husband's getting for Father's Day.

– Miranda, Mountain View CA

UNDER 30 MINUTES

A local pizza place in our town boasts the best pizza around, plus fast delivery. They are so confident in their delivery time that they'll give their customers the pizza for free if it's not there within 30 minutes.

My husband Shane has taken this policy way, way too far and made it his goal in life to never again pay for a pizza.

Shane has developed a few methods for ensuring that the pizza restaurant will never, ever make a delivery to our house within the 30-minute window.

First, he makes sure that he only orders pizza during the busiest possible times such as 7:00 pm on a Friday night or right before halftime on Super Bowl Sunday. He'll also make difficult, custom pizza orders to ensure that it takes the restaurant longer to cook and deliver his pizza. For instance, he'll ask for a pepperoni-cheese pizza with green olives only on half of the pizza and mushrooms and onions on the other half. Then he'll ask that one half of the pizza be well done and crispy, while the other half is soft and gooey. This way, if the pizza delivery man should somehow manage to make it to our door within 30 minutes, there's a good chance my husband can claim that they've got his order wrong, and use that as a justification for a free pizza.

My husband's orders are so confusing that half the time I'm not sure even he understands them.

My husband further buys himself more time by leaving our rottweiler tied up to our front porch when he orders a pizza. The pizza man will be forced to deal with this additional obstacle in order to make it to our door within 30 minutes. Shane might as well get a moat full of alligators dug across our front lawn.

Sometimes he will intentionally give the pizza deliveryman the next-door neighbor's address instead of our own. My husband will wait until the very last second when the pizza man is fed up and about to leave before he speaks up and claims the pizza.

"Hey! There you are," my husband will yell.
"I've been waiting for you for
31 minutes!"

"He has delivery down to a science."

The last time that my husband tried to pull the "next-door neighbor" trick, it backfired on him. Because he had placed such a difficult order this time and it took so long to cook, by the time our pizza got to the neighbor's door, it was already well past the point where they could try and charge for it. Rather than rejecting the free pizza, our neighbor knew better than to look a gift pizza in the mouth.

He paid the deliveryman a tip and took the pizza inside to enjoy!

I found my husband standing by the window, watching the whole incident unfold. "That bastard!" my husband said. "He took our pizza!"

"Well, you can try to order another one," I told my cheap hubby. "But I'm going out to get Chinese."

– Terri, Orange CA

51

DUCT TAPE REPAIRMAN

Early in our relationship, my first husband Wally raved about his handyman talents– how he could fix anything, anywhere, anytime. I believe I might have married him on that promise alone. My mother used to say that if a man was good in the sack and came with a set of tools, you were set for life. What Mom neglected to mention was, like sex, you might want to try before you buy, and actually open the toolbox to see what's inside.

The "repairs" started out with a little piece of duct tape to hold the bottom of the toaster together, so that every time it heated up, miniscule plastic fumes would permeate my toast until I ripped it out of the wall and bought a new one. I like peanut butter on my toast– not hazardous waste. We fought about that for days.

Then I found duct tape at the bottom of a table leg to keep it from wobbling, a larger piece on the bookshelf that held all of his do-it-yourself books (that's a laugh), and another strip holding the refrigerator together. Within one year, the cheap bastard had duct-taped everything we owned so that our house now resembled a kind of creepy, silver spider web.

As often as I would replace an old item with a new version, Wally would discover a "flaw" and immediately secure it with tape.

It's always been such a source of arguments between us, but, somehow, he always persuaded me that it was worth it, because of the money we saved. And I always ended up giving in.

Last month, our dog Siesta came into the house through his doggie door, limping around as if his leg was really causing him pain. I wanted to immediately take him to our vet (who I really liked), just in case he had been hit by a car. But Wally insisted we wait just one day, in case it was nothing serious.

The next afternoon, I arrived home from work, anxious to see what Siesta's condition was.

Wally looked up from his newspaper. "Hi, honey," he told me with a big smile on his face. "Siesta has received medical attention and is good as new."

"Where is he?" I asked.
"He's in his doggie bed," he informed me.

"Man's best friend"

I slowly walked over to the corner of the living room to Siesta's bed. He'd been so quiet, I didn't even realize he was there. When I got closer to him, I saw what kind of medical attention he'd received.....his leg was covered in duct tape! The poor thing looked up at me as if to say, "Please help!"

Well, that was five years ago, and things are very different now. Siesta is completely recovered now, after receiving proper medical attention from that veterinarian that I liked so much. As a matter of fact, he liked me too. We're married now.

As for my former husband Wally.....he's happily working at the downtown hardware store. Increasing their sales of duct tape, no doubt.

– Angela. Dallas TX

52

CAUGHT NAKED

During the winter, I bundle up in a thermal undershirt and a sweater, with a scarf wrapped around my neck. Unfortunately, it's not because I'm going anywhere. I do it because my cheap husband Rick wants to save money and won't turn on the heat! I could be shivering down to my bones inside the house and he'll sit there and be totally fine with it.

We live in Las Vegas, and what's worse than winter is the summer. During the unbearable summer months, it will be scorching hot outside and my cheap husband refuses to turn on the air conditioner. We're baking like turkeys in an oven, while everyone else is relaxing in the comforts of their air-conditioned homes.

One summer day, when it was 95 degrees outside, it felt like it was 110 degrees inside the house. My husband still wouldn't turn on the air conditioner! So, when he left to go to the grocery store, I decided to take off all my clothes and lie face down naked on our floor in the middle of the living room to keep cool. My son was spending the day at the pool with his friends, so I had the house to myself.

Although I wasn't thrilled about having to resort to nudity to keep cool, not having clothing on sure was a relief to me. I felt so relaxed that I fell asleep.

The next thing I knew, there were three firemen busting through the front door and standing over my bare body.

Apparently, the nosy next-door neighbor had been peeking over the fence and saw me naked lying on the floor. She called 9-1-1, afraid that I might have fallen and been knocked unconscious.

A few minutes later, when my husband came home to find me wrapped in a towel, and laughing about the incident with three handsome firemen, he wasn't too happy. But he soon decided that running the A/C is probably a good idea.

– Marcy, Las Vegas NV

My Husband the Cheap Bastard Test
HOW CHEAP IS YOUR HUSBAND?

Check off everything that is applicable to your spouse. When you're finished, count everything up and determine your cheap bastard percentage.

- [ ] He hoards plastic bags from the supermarket
- [ ] He uses coupon and discount cards for all his purchases
- [ ] He returns gifts to the store for cash
- [ ] He rarely tips or tips less than 10 percent
- [ ] He buys "Secret Santa" presents at the dollar store
- [ ] He always asks to split the bill
- [ ] He brings his own food into the movie theater
- [ ] He reuses wrapping paper on presents
- [ ] He attends art openings strictly for the food and wine
- [ ] His idea of a nice gift is a birthday card
- [ ] He makes meals out of the free samples in the grocery store
- [ ] He returns his restaurant meal after devouring half of it
- [ ] He uses electronics and returns them before warranty expires
- [ ] He buys the cheapest toilet paper available
- [ ] He asks family members to chip in for Thanksgiving dinner
- [ ] He has an illegal cable hookup
- [ ] He stocks his pantry with free fast-food condiment packets
- [ ] He photocopies books from front to back
- [ ] He returns books after reading them
- [ ] He overstocks items, even ones he doesn't need
- [ ] He clips "buy one, get one free" coupons
- [ ] He haggles stores employees for discounts
- [ ] He reuses soda cups for free refills at restaurants
- [ ] He buys oversized clothes for his kids so they'll last longer
- [ ] He makes meals out of happy-hour food
- [ ] He brings outside food into restaurants
- [ ] He takes home food from buffets
- [ ] He uses duct tape for repairs
- [ ] He refuses to turn on the AC or heater because it's expensive
- [ ] His favorite stores are dollar stores
- [ ] He creates counterfeit hole-punches for coffee/video/carwash card

- [ ] He crashes on sofas to avoid paying for hotels
- [ ] He takes back tips left on the table
- [ ] He sneaks from movie to movie in multiplexes
- [ ] He rushes you off the phone mid-conservation to stay within allotted cell-phone minutes
- [ ] He returns outfits after wearing them
- [ ] He parks five blocks away to avoid paying for parking
- [ ] He avoids flushing the toilet to save money on water use
- [ ] He commits mail fraud in order to save money on postage
- [ ] He will drive around for hours looking for cheap gas
- [ ] He tells the kids Santa will come after Christmas, so he can take advantage of post-holiday sales
- [ ] He'd rather eat the free birthday meals at restaurants than the one you prepared for him
- [ ] He brings his own beverages to restaurants
- [ ] He lies about his kids' age to get the child's ticket prices
- [ ] He steals company supplies for the home
- [ ] He borrows the neighbor's newspaper and returns after reading it
- [ ] He buys expired or old products at reduced prices
- [ ] He wastes countless hours on the Internet surfing for deals
- [ ] He purchases flowers in a grocery store rather than paying a florist
- [ ] He dumpster-dives and seeks out garage sales for bargains
- [ ] He will dream up/forge an imaginary price-match challenge at electronics stores
- [ ] He signs up for trial subscriptions and cancels them before the trial ends
- [ ] He joins and re-joins online services under different names to avoid paying fees
- [ ] He brings his own wine into a restaurant
- [ ] He borrows unused bandwidth from afar via wireless networking
- [ ] He snacks on bulk candy and grapes in the supermarket
- [ ] He takes you to a diner, and shares a cup of coffee with you
- [ ] He camps out at buffet restaurants through two meals
- [ ] He buys himself tickets online for "student or seniors" at a reduced price
- [ ] He eats the same thing for a week in order to save a buck

SCORE

0 – 5	Let it go. We all have our little quirks.
6 – 10	You'd better keep him in check before it gets more serious.
11 – 20	Yep.....you've got a cheapskate on your hands, but it could always be worse.
21 – 30	Schedule an appointment with the therapist.
31 +	Got a good divorce lawyer?

→
TO OUR READERS

Retired Hipster publishes books on topics ranging from personal growth to artistic expression to relationships. Our mission is to put out quality books that celebrate expression and nourish the human spirit – such as visual explosions in art, design and photography, as well as a full line of journals and gifts that will inspire you, make you laugh, and breathe new vitality into your life. We value integrity, compassion, and receptivity both in the books we publish and in the way we do business.

Our readers are our most important resource, and we value your suggestions, input, and ideas about what you would like to see published. Please feel free to contact us, to request our latest book catalog, or to be added to our mailing list.

Retired Hipster, Inc.
PO Box 14068
San Francisco, CA 94114
www.retiredhipster.com